The Joplin Tornado

House of Hope

AKA "The Volunteer House"

by:

Tim A. Bartow

The Joplin Tornado

House of Hope

AKA "The Volunteer House"

by:

Tim A. Bartow

Printed in the Unites States of America
First Printing: February 2012
ISBN: 978-1441435651

A production of MAXnJAX Media

For more information, please visit: www.jthoh.com

Acknowledgments

First of all, I would like to express my gratitude to my Heavenly Father for bringing my family, friends, neighbors, and me safely through the storm. In light of the incredibly destructive power of the tornado, it is nothing short of a miracle that there were so few deaths and injuries. This experience reinforced to us what is really important in life.

My wife, Stacey, knows how much I love and adore her, but I can never tell her often enough. She is my soulmate and I am blessed beyond measure to have her in my life. Throughout all of our many sufferings, hardships, trials, and tribulations, she has been amazingly supportive and strong, always by my side.

I'm greatly blessed to have the love and support of a wonderful family. No matter what happens in life, it's reassuring to know that family will always be there to catch us when we fall. I couldn't have hand picked a better group of people with whom to share life.

I am honored to have such good and faithful friends who also provide a great deal of support and assistance in our lives. My family and I have been blessed beyond measure to have made many hundreds more friends since the tornado.

I would like to thank all of my new friends who helped bring this story to print. Whether in your actions or words, you have shown me the true meaning of charity... the true love of Christ, and I am forever grateful to know you and to have shared so many wonderful experiences with you. You inspire me!

A special thanks to everyone who contributed photos, artwork, lyrics, poetry, stories, and other insights. Your contributions were perfect for this book and they are greatly appreciated.

A big hug to my friends and family members who were so capable, willing, and available on short notice to proof read my manuscript, providing me with the many suggestions that were necessary to make this book a better read.

My sincere appreciation and gratitude to each and every person who helped not only the community of Joplin, but in communities everywhere that suffer any type of tragedy. Their suffering is no different from ours and any help, thoughts, or prayers offered in their behalf are a blessing to all of us who share this planet!

And finally, many thanks to you, the reader, for allowing me to share a such an amazing story with you, your family, and friends.

Dedication

This book is dedicated to the countless volunteers who selflessly and lovingly served the community of Joplin and the surrounding area after the tragic destruction of the EF5 tornado on 5-22-2011.

Whether you were one of the people who helped save a person's life, or one of the people who provided medical care and attention, or one of the people who dug through our rubble and debris, or one of the people who prepared one of the many sack lunches or other meals we ate, or one of the people who helped make a quilt, or one of the people who wrote a poem, painted a picture, sang a song, or made a video to encourage us, or one of the people who helped build or rebuild something destroyed, or one of the people who provided refreshments, or one of the people who brought us water, particle masks, and work gloves, or one of the people who moved a house piece by piece, or one of the people who cut down trees, or one of the people who handed out money or gift cards, or one of the people who provided pain, muscle and joint relief, or one of the people who sent cards and letters of support and love, or one of the people who donated time, money, resources, or materials, or one of the people who donated or delivered clothing and household goods, or one of the people who manned the various relief centers, or one of the people who gave aid to our pets, or one of the people who rescued our lost documents and photographs, or one of the people who washed dirty laundry for others, of one of the people who took in a stranger and gave them a place to sleep, or one of the people who helped with the assembly and distribution of personal hygiene kits and care packages, or one of the people who provided heavy equipment and tools, or one of the people who were moved to action and helped in any way – big or small, or one of the people who simply prayed with us or for us, or one of the companies who donated time, money, resources, or materials to ease the suffering of our residents... you helped us heal and move forward in many ways, and you are the inspiration and the reason for this book.

On that fateful evening, those of us affected by the tornado did not have a choice about whether we wanted to be in Joplin or not. Our only choices were "upstairs / downstairs," or "bathtub / closet," or "this wall / that wall," or something similar.

On the other hand, each and every volunteer who touched our lives in any way, did have a choice. The fact that they chose to come to our aid in our darkest hour will forever make them our heroes, and we will be forever grateful for each and every one of them and the contribution they made, no matter how big or how small.

The faith, hope, and love manifested by those volunteers are the epitome of the Master's admonition;

> *For I was an hungered and ye gave me meat: I was thirsty, and ye gave me drink: I was a stranger, and ye took me in: Naked, and ye clothed me: I was sick, and ye visited me.*
>
> *Then shall the righteous answer him, saying, Lord, when saw we thee an hungered, and fed thee? Or thirsty, and gave thee drink? When saw we thee a stranger, and took thee in? Or naked, and clothed thee?*
>
> *And the King shall answer and say unto them, Inasmuch as ye have done it unto one of the least of these my brethren, ye have done it unto me.*

When I contemplate the gratitude I feel (and I think I represent the community), I struggle with the words to adequately convey the feelings that cause my heart to swell when I think of all those who gave so much for us. Even though it seems inadequate, I wrote it once, and I'll keep writing it every time I get the chance...

THANK YOU VOLUNTEERS WE ♥ U! YOU ARE OUR HEROES!!

Preface

The following story is told through the eyes of those who experienced the destruction and rejuvenation of Joplin firsthand. It is the story of my family and our interactions with various volunteers and others who have forever changed our lives and inspired us. Their individual stories are woven into our story and reveal the emotions from both the givers and the receivers, of the compassion and service so freely rendered.

Even though the individual stories in this book represent a small fraction of the people who served in Joplin, I believe they epitomize the quality of character, heart, and soul of all those who volunteered or contributed in any way.

As a result of the tornado's devastation, more than one hundred sixty people lost their lives, with the injured numbering more than a thousand. More than eighteen thousand vehicles were destroyed and nearly seven thousand homes lost, with nearly a thousand more damaged. There were nearly five hundred businesses leveled or damaged, many of them medical facilities, affecting more than five thousand jobs. The high school was decimated along with five other school buildings and seven more damaged. One of the two main hospitals in the four state area took a direct hit along with a nearby nursing home, destroying both. Several churches along the path of the tornado were also destroyed.

Because of the staggering array of tragic statistics, it would be easy to see the events of that fateful Sunday as a tale of destruction, disparity, and death. Even though these statistics and tragedy are certainly a part of the events, I am convinced that the story that will be forever told will be one of the extreme outpouring and manifestation of faith, hope, and love.

The people who were monitoring and following the storm activity that day will tell you that the conditions were perfect for a devastating tornado. I am convinced that the conditions following the storm were perfect for a miracle. Not just one miracle, but countless miracles, the likes of which we have never before witnessed or experienced.

The real story has less to do with damage, disparity, destruction, and death, and more to do with preservation, rebuilding, and healing. It's about renewed hope and faith, healed hearts and lives, spiritual and emotional growth, perseverance and determination, charity and compassion. It is the power of love, a story of triumph, and the miracle of the human spirit... the very heart of America!

"There are incalculable resources in the human spirit, once it has been set free."
- Hubert H. Humphrey

"I am certain that after the dust of centuries has passed over our cities, we, too, will be remembered not for victories or defeats in battles or in politics, but for our contribution to the human spirit."
- John Fitzgerald Kennedy

"The human heart, even after this, remains stronger than this very ground."
- Anonymous
(written on kitchen floor tiles)

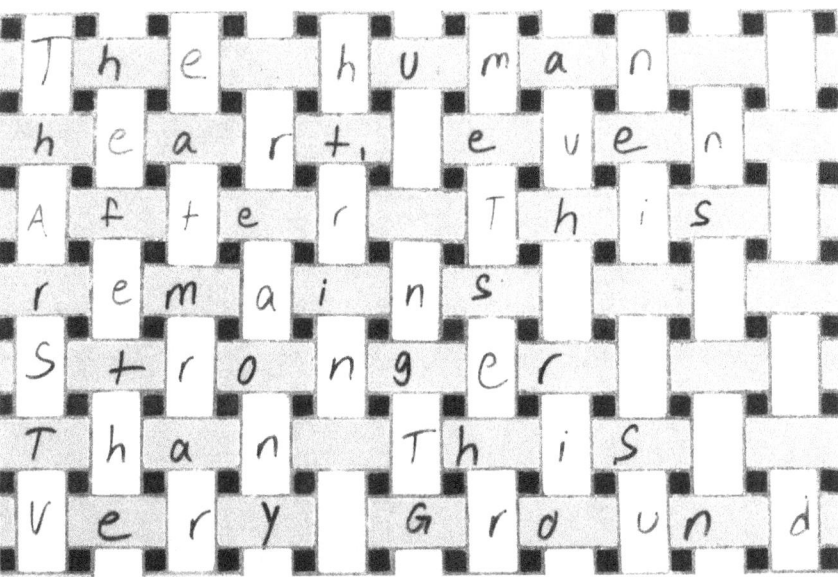

Chapter 1

This Sunday was not unlike any other Sunday in Southwest Missouri. My wife, Stacey, and I got up early and started fixing breakfast for our family. Our clan consisted of us, our two daughters, Abby (seventeen years old and six months pregnant), and Heather (fifteen years old).

We were joined that morning by Abby's friend, Taylor, and the pilgrims who lived in the house next door. No, "pilgrim" was not their name, but rather my nickname for them. The pilgrims consisted of my daughter, Tiffany, her husband, Adam, and their two daughters, Grace (two and a half years old), and Olivia (two months old).

Pilgrim is a term used in the old west and popularized in some old John Wayne movies and in the Clint Eastwood movie, "The Outlaw Josie Wales." Pilgrim referred to any tender footed person who was unprepared for a sojourn in the unchartered and oftentimes dangerous wild west. Like most young couples just starting out, they lacked the experience and wisdom that can only be gained over time through "the school of hard knocks."

Our Sunday morning breakfast consisted of pancakes along with country fried potatoes with onions and bell peppers jazzed up with some spices. We also included a big pan of fried ham and scrambled eggs with cheese all mixed together. To round out the meal, we had some biscuits and country gravy with sausage.

This morning was a little different because we included an additional item to our breakfast. The previous day, Grace and I had been out picking fresh strawberries from our five foot wide and forty foot long strawberry patch. We already had a couple of gallons of beautifully ripe berries that, along with some whipped cream, would compliment our standard breakfast fare quite nicely.

Sitting at the dining room table enjoying our breakfast feast the conversation centered around this year's gardening activities.

"The zucchini, yellow squash, and cucumbers are all coming up nicely," I announced. "It will be fun for Grace to watch them grow, since she helped me plant them."

Grace with a strawberry in her hand and lots of juice all over her face

Grace and I had planted the seeds two weeks earlier. I anticipated having a lot of fun with her this summer, tending to the plants and then eating the vegetables as they matured. It would be a good learning experience for her, so she could see how food grows and the concept of "reaping what you sew."

I could see in my mind's eye the pictures I would take with her standing next to the big mature plants and vines, imagining how proud she would be of herself, gardening with Grandpa.

She was my gardening buddy, always anxious and willing to help water the plants, dig in the dirt, put the seeds in the ground, etc.

More than anything, she absolutely loved to go out every morning to pick and eat fresh fruit. With all the fruit trees, bushes, and plants, we had fresh fruit from May through October. There was always some fruit that was in season, just waiting to be picked and enjoyed.

Grace watering blueberry
plants with Grandpa

"Hey, Beautiful, can you please pass me the syrup," I asked Stacey, spreading a chunk of melting butter over my fluffy, steaming hot pancakes.

"I've got another batch of giant strawberries on order that should be here any day," I said. "Some of the ever-bearing strawberries didn't survive over the winter, so I'm going to plant the giant berries toward the front of the house."

"We're going to Lowe's and Home Depot this week to pick out a couple of fruit trees," Tiffany chimed in, "will you help us get them planted?"

"Sure, but you're going to need to pick up some bags of manure, top soil, and fertilizer while you're at it. Let's try to get it done the next day Adam has off. I'm going to need him to do the lion's share of the grunt work of digging the holes and getting all the big rocks out of your ground."

During the past three years, I had transformed our place into a miniature fruit orchard and berry farm. We had two apple trees,

3

two pear trees, two plum trees, and three peach trees.

There was the big strawberry patch running along the south side of the house with four rhubarb plants near the back deck.

Scattered throughout the back yard there were eight blackberry bushes, eight raspberry bushes, five blueberry bushes, two goji bushes, a cherry bush, a current bush, and a gooseberry bush.

We had a dozen grape vines of various varieties that covered the fence around the back yard.

Tiffany picking strawberries - rhubarb plants in upper left of photo

Not being satisfied with my own back yard, I had convinced the pilgrims to follow my lead and we had transformed their back yard into a similar "farmer's market."

We were especially excited about our harvest this year because it was the first year that every single plant was going to bear fruit, including the grapes. I had just finished pruning all the vines a few weeks earlier and there were perfect little grape clusters all along the fences in both yards.

"By the way, are we still on for pulled pork tacos at your place tonight?" I asked Tiffany.

"Absolutely," she replied confidently, "the pork roast is in the crock pot, even as we speak."

Tiffany had been to dinner at a friend's house where she enjoyed eating some pulled pork tacos. She had raved about them for weeks and how deliciously wonderful they were. The only natural thing to do, it seemed to me, was to challenge her to get the recipe and make them for the rest of the family.

After breakfast, our attention turned to getting everyone ready for church. The pilgrims went next door and the rest of us put away the breakfast things, washed the dishes, and changed into our dress clothes for church services.

Church didn't start until 1:00 p.m., which was good for me since I also like to sleep in whenever I get the chance. Sunday service ended at 4:00 p.m., which basically shot the day for doing much of anything else. However, it did facilitate a good amount of time for a big breakfast and an even bigger dinner.

We got back from church around 4:15 and pulled up to the back gate, just beyond the large wooden deck at the back of the house. The pilgrims were just pulling up to their house when I stepped out onto the concrete driveway.

"Hey," I yelled as Tiffany was climbing out of their car, "what time do you want us to come over?"

"Be here by six," she shouted back.

We raced inside the house and quickly changed into something more comfortable. For us, that was sweat pants and t-shirts.

Abby, Taylor, and Heather went to their separate rooms where they began the ritual of texting their friends and adding comments on their social network sites.

I went into the kitchen and called our two dogs to the back yard, so they could "do their business." Maxine (we called her Max) was the oldest at two and a half years old and weighing in at about five pounds. She was half Chihuahua and half Yorkie, making her a "Chorkie." Jaxon was a year and a half old, a purebred Yorkie weighing in at about ten pounds.

They say that once in a lifetime a pet owner will get one truly remarkable pet, and for me it was Max. She's incredibly smart, especially when considering how tiny her brain is. Jaxon, on the other hand got the good looks, but was passed up for a brain. One of the sweetest dogs I've ever seen, but dumber than a fence post.

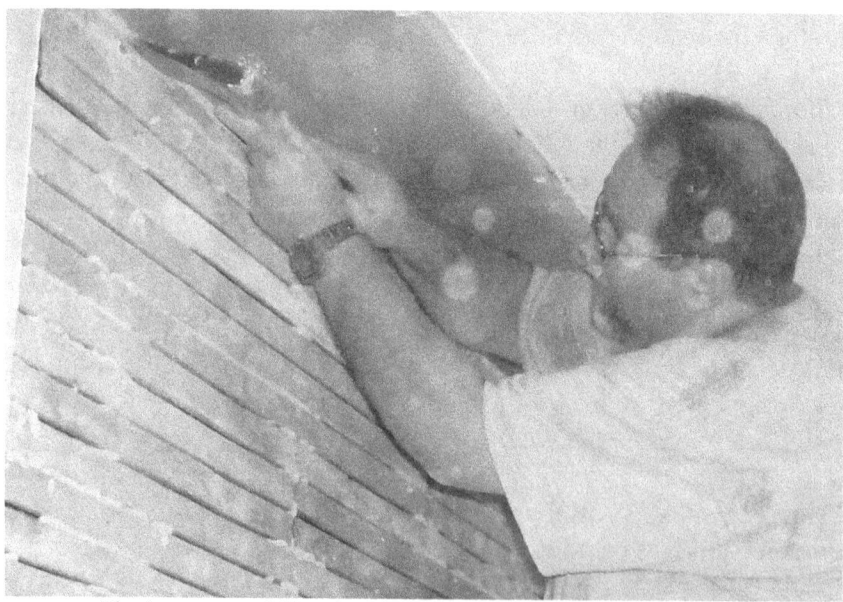

That's me remodeling the kitchen, chipping away at the plaster

Being outside with the dogs, waiting for them to finish their business, I wandered around, checking on the various plants and trees to see if they might need any insecticide or fungicide. I also performed my daily ritual of picking off the Japanese beetles that seemed to have infested our neighborhood. As I was making my plant inspection rounds, Stacey walked out the back door.

"I'm going to sweep the bricks one last time," she announced, picking up a straw broom that lay propped against the concrete, between the steps and the deck.

"That's perfect," I said, "and then we'll finally be done with all the landscaping!"

For the five and a half years we lived in the house, we had devoted our extra time and resources to remodeling it. It was a three bedroom, one bath Craftsman style house that was built in the early nineteen-twenties, making it about ninety years old.

It had lots of hardwood throughout, from floor to ceiling. It had beautiful, one inch wide oak hardwood floors that you can't even buy these days. It was finished with fir baseboards, door and window jams, solid wood doors, real crystal door knobs, brass hinges and skeleton key locks. The kitchen and bathroom floors were individually hand laid pieces of Egyptian marble tiles in a basket weave pattern.

When we first moved in, the floors in every room were covered with carpet from the sixties and seventies. The kitchen and bathroom floors were covered with indoor/outdoor carpet from decades past that had been glued to the tile.

Once we started taking up the carpets, we found another layer of carpet (used as padding) that predated the carpet on top by a decade or two. Once we got the carpets and padding pulled up, it was as though the floors had been locked in a time capsule, having been preserved for the past fifty or sixty years.

7

Over those years of remodeling, it went from being just an old house to what you might consider a dear friend. By the time we had completely refinished and remodeled most of the house, it was a part of our lives and we knew every inch of it intimately.

Sure, it had its quirks, but then again so do all of our family members. Most people would say it was just an old house, but you could never have convinced Stacey or me of that. To us, it was part of the family.

"I think I'm finished," Stacey said, standing on the sidewalk with broom in hand, admiring her handiwork.

"It looks good," I said, walking up next to her, wrapping my arm around her shoulder, "you did a great job."

We stood there for a few minutes, admiring the finished brick project, relishing the thought that we were finally finished with both the inside remodeling and the outside landscaping.

Stacey had been pestering me for the past couple of years to do some landscaping around the house. I kept putting her off, telling her that I would start on it once we got the fruit trees, bushes, and garden in the ground and well established.

This was the year for the landscaping since all of the "farmer's market" planting had been completed. This summer had been dedicated for beautifying the property. We had spent most of the spring doing landscaping and planting ornamental plants around the front of the house and replanting some in the back yard.

The very last project was to dig up and "brick in" a section of ground between the sidewalk and driveway. I had put this project off until last because it was going to be a pain in the back.

It involved digging up rose bushes and other flowering plants, and replanting them somewhere else in the yard. Then we would have to dig up several wheelbarrows full of dirt and rocks to get down far enough for the brick to fit at the same height as the sidewalk and driveway.

The stove, exhaust hood, and kitchen area after remodeling

The bricks we laid were still in place after the tornado

We finally finished on Saturday, the previous day. Once we got the bricks laid in place, we poured sand all over the bricks and swept it into the spaces between them.

Once the sand was spread over the bricks, we sprayed water over the area so the sand could settle between the bricks When done properly, it looks like a brick wall on the ground.

"Let's walk around the house and admire the fruits of our labors," I said, squeezing Stacey's shoulder.

She stepped onto the bricks and set the broom down, leaning it against the concrete between the steps and the deck. Taking my hand we walked around the entire house, commenting on various aspects of the plants and how each one made our home and property better in their own way.

We walked across the street, turned around and stood there for several minutes admiring our work. Much had been accomplished over the past five years and if was a relief to finally be done. We were pleased with our home and how perfect it was for our family.

At that moment, a feeling came over us that can only be described by one of those "homey, feel good, Hallmark Christmas cards" where all the world is at peace.

Walking across the street, around to the back of the house, the wind began to stir up a gentle, cooling breeze. Max and Jaxon ran to meet us at the gate, excitedly jumping up and down.

"Let's go inside," I called to them and they headed straight for the back door.

Once inside, I went to our bedroom and sitting down at the desk, turned on my computer.

"We need to proof read some chapters of your book," I yelled out to Stacey, "I think I've made all the changes you wanted."

"Okay," she hollered back, "I'll be there in just a minute."

Stacey had been the Director of Nursing at a long term care facility for the past five years and wanted to write a book that covered various aspects of leadership and working with people in the healthcare industry. I helped her by doing the typing, artwork, and layout for the book. She was ready to send the manuscript to the publisher, but had made some last minute changes that needed a final review for accuracy and content.

"Dad," Abby said excitedly, running down the hallway, bursting into our bedroom, "Taylor's mom just called and said she has to go home because there's a tornado headed this way."

Taylor lived several blocks away from us in a northwesterly

direction. She was certain that her mother knew what she was talking about and was anxious to get home.

"Well, let's go take a look before we get all panicked," I said, stepping away from the desk, "I doubt there's a tornado headed this way. They usually drop down in Oklahoma or Kansas and miss us altogether."

North side of kitchen after remodeling

"What's going on?" Stacey asked as she appeared from the living room, "who saw a tornado?"

"There's no tornado," I assured her, walking toward the back door, "Taylor's mom is just worried and wants her to come home."

Stepping onto the back steps, the wind had picked up and was gusting about twenty to twenty-five miles per hour. In this part of the country wind speeds like that are not uncommon and often much stronger. Just the year before, we had straight line winds of eighty to ninety miles per hour and all it did was knock down a few trees, lots of branches, and scattered garbage cans everywhere.

Unfortunately, one of the trees that did fall that day, had a branch that landed on my beautiful 1984 Dodge Ram Prospector short bed pickup truck and dinged the cab. That tree had already been cut up for firewood, so there was one less tree to worry about falling over.

"See, the wind's not even blowing that hard," I argued, "it blows a lot harder than this when it rains... this is nothing."

"I've got to take Taylor home now," Abby insisted, as they raced down the steps and across the yard to where Abby's car was parked, "I'll be right back!"

"I need to check the TV and see if there's anything going on," Stacey said, hurrying inside the house.

Standing there on the deck by myself, I thought back on my life, having grown up in "tornado alley." I lived where tornadoes had hit and seen the damage they caused. In all my experience with tornadoes, unless you were in the direct path of the vortex, any property damage suffered would, in all likelihood, be sustainable and recoverable. *Besides*, I reasoned, *we have a basement and we can take cover downstairs if there really is a tornado.*

When I was about to return to the house, I noticed that the sky was turning a green color off in the distance. I remember many years ago when I lived in Texas and a tornado had touched down near our neighborhood. One of my friends, Michelle, commented that the sky always turned green before a tornado.

I had always dismissed that notion since I couldn't reason in my mind what atmospheric conditions it would take to turn the sky green. Gray or even black I could understand, but who ever heard of *green* skies?

I'm still not buying it, I thought, *but I'll go inside and check out the radar images on the internet to see for myself.*

"Baby, there are tornado warnings all over the TV," Stacey blurted out as I walked through the back door, "I'm scared!"

The skies were angry above and around Joplin for several days

Stacey had grown up in Florida where they have hurricanes all the time. She wasn't accustomed to this, whereas I grew up watching TV as tornado warnings scrolled across the bottom of the screen and not giving it much thought.

If the wind wasn't blowing hard enough to shake your house, you didn't have anything to worry about. Living in tornado alley you get used to the overzealous weather people and even the national weather service. I clearly had become immune to such warnings.

"You lived in Florida," I argued, "they have hurricanes there all the time and they sometimes spawn tornadoes."

"Yeah, but you know they're coming for days or weeks in advance

14

and you have time to leave the area if you want!"

"Don't stress out, I'm going to look on the radar right now and we'll see if there's anything to worry about."

I sat down at my computer and pulled up a radar image of our area. The time on the image was almost fifteen minutes earlier, but I could see that there was a major storm almost on top of us. There was a deep, dark red circle right in the middle of the storm. Looking at the color scale, it was the darkest color on the scale.

Without a doubt, I thought, *we're in for one ugly thunderstorm.*

Just then, the tornado warning siren began to blare. I looked out the window to check conditions. The sky was getting darker but I couldn't see anything worthy of being a tornado. The trees weren't bent over, there were no funnel clouds, no hail... not even any rain!

Our old house spoke to us in a language of its own. We could tell by the creaks, cracks, and groans what was going on and where, inside and out. We could hear the water running through the old steel pipes every time someone turned on the water or flushed the toilet. We could hear the heater, air conditioner, and water heater turning on and off.

When the wind blew more than a breeze, the old windows rattled in their hardwood frames. In fact, we could tell how hard the wind was blowing just by the speed the windows were rattling. At this point, the windows weren't rattling at all.

Still, just to be on the safe side, I went back to my computer and refreshed the radar map to see if there was a more recent image. When the screen refreshed, it was the same image as before and had not updated with a newer image.

"There's a tornado coming," Abby yelled as she came charging through the back door, "Taylor's mom said they've spotted one west of us and it's headed right this way!"

At that moment complete and total bedlam broke loose in our home with "Chicken Little" leading the craziness. It was complete and frenzied chaos to say the least. Everyone was running around the house yelling "tornado, tornado... get to the basement!"

Still not convinced, I went out to the back deck to see if there really was something to all these warnings. Things still did not look that bad to me. Abby came racing out of the house and ran over to the pilgrims' house, disappearing through their back door. And then there was silence.

The tornado warning siren that had been blaring for the previous couple of minutes stopped, and there was silence. *Another false alarm*, I thought, *just like all the other false alarms before*.

We didn't know the siren had been knocked out of service by the tornado

With the threat of a tornado gone, I went back into the bedroom and began shutting down the computer and all the other electronics. I figured there was a pretty good chance of a very severe thunderstorm which always included lightning. In our neck of the woods, lightning more often than not, resulted in power surges and outages which are never good for electronic devices.

16

Stacey had her notebook computer powered on and there were TVs turned on throughout the house. I started yelling, "turn off the electronics" to everyone in the house. They were completely ignoring me, yelling back to get down in the basement as they disappeared around the corner and down the stairs.

Are you kidding me, I thought, *I guess I'll have to turn everything off myself.*

Just then, Abby and the pilgrims come running through the back door, across the kitchen with my two granddaughters in tow, headed straight for the basement.

"Get downstairs!" Adam yelled, running past me and following the others down the stairs into the basement.

Why, you sissy, I was thinking, *you're running downstairs with the women and children and I need you to get back up here and help with the electronics.*

All of a sudden, without any warning, not even the slightest rattling of the windows, it was as if someone had set off explosives outside every window in the house, blowing them to pieces.

Our bedroom was located on the southwest corner of the house. About half of the surface area of the south and west walls was big picture windows.

I was still sitting at my desk with my back to the west when the windows exploded. I heard a thunderous roaring, the shattering of glass, and metal mini blinds twisting and tearing. Rain and debris of every kind blasted through the empty window frames as if shot from a cannon, pummeling me and crashing all around as the power failed and the house suddenly went dark.

I don't believe it, I thought as total panic surged through me and the adrenaline began pumping, *there really is a tornado!*

My niece, Ashley, outside the bedroom window that exploded on me

I raced as fast as I could down the short hallway, past the bathroom and through the kitchen. Grabbing the wall by the stairwell leading to the basement, I swung myself around the corner and through the doorway.

Starting down the stairs, I could see the kitchen walls being ripped away from the house and debris was flying everywhere. I went down the stairs so fast that I only hit the edge of a couple of the steps and just about busted my butt when I hit the floor.

At the bottom of the stairs, my family was all huddled together in the center of the basement. I did a quick count of who should be there. All the humans were present and accounted for. Heather was holding Jaxon, but I didn't see Max anywhere.

"Where's Max, who's got Max?" I yelled, knowing that the dog house was in the kitchen, which at that very moment was being ripped apart. Having just witnessed the kitchen walls being dismantled, I knew there was no way she could survive up there.

"We've got her," Stacey assured me, "where do we need to go to be safe from the tornado?"

I made a quick assessment of the basement from where we were standing. The basement wasn't so much a regular basement as it was originally a garage under the house. The flimsy sixteen foot wide, tinny garage door on the west side was already giving way and debris was shooting through, whipping around in the air.

"Everybody get behind here," I yelled, leading them to the east side of the basement.

The chimney for the original coal fired heating system was still standing strong. Clustered around the chimney was the central heat and air conditioning system and the water heater. There was a steel I-beam that ran the length of the house next to the chimney that supported the center of the house.

I figured this area of the basement would be the most structurally sound location and out of the direct path of the debris blasting through the garage door. We all gathered and huddled together with the pilgrims hovering over the children.

In times of crisis, people tend to either have their minds go totally blank, becoming confused and panicked or they accelerate into complete clarity and focus. Fortunately, I'm blessed with the clarity and focus type of mind, so I began evaluating our risk factors relative to the tornado.

From my personal experience, I felt pretty confident that unless we were in the direct path of the vortex and the area immediately around it, we were probably going to be okay and I didn't need to worry about any of us dying right then.

Max & Jaxon's custom built dog house / kitchen cabinet

People often describe the sound of a tornado as that of a roaring locomotive. I will disagree with that, because it sounded like a dozen roaring locomotives. It may have sounded like one locomotive off in the distance, but by the time it was on top of us, it was deafening!

I was in such a hurry to get down the stairs that I didn't take the time to close the door behind me, so it was flapping back and forth. The garage door was being ripped out of it's tracks and a couple of the basement windows had shattered. When you consider that the kitchen walls were missing, we had a pretty good opportunity to hear the tornado in all its fury, up close and personal.

All this time I kept thinking that the chances of us being in the direct path were slim. I hoped that we were off to one side or the other. I also hoped that it would be a less powerful tornado that only did minimal damage and wouldn't totally destroy the house. *Could we be that lucky*, I wondered as the roaring became louder.

Because of the way our old house was built, it wasn't sound proof in any sense of the word. We could hear people talking from any adjoining room or down in the basement, almost as if we were in the same room.

As the roaring grew louder, we could hear the turbulent crashing and crunching of building materials hitting the hardwood floor that was just a few feet above our heads. *Thank God we've got solid hardwood floors,* I thought, trying to reassure myself, *and that steel I-beam above us to keep anything from breaking through the floor on top of us.*

At this time, I wasn't really scared for our safety. I knew there would be damage to the house and our vehicles, but I never felt in danger of losing my life or any of my family members. Instead, I was strangely interested in the sounds and other sensory aspects of the tornado. I listened intently to the chaotic clatter of destruction, making observations and mental notes of my surroundings constantly. I suppose my science teachers would all be proud of my scientific approach to the disaster.

Before long, the roaring and crunching subsided and was replaced by a loud groaning and creaking. If you've ever pulled a big, long nail from a piece of wood and it creaks and groans, you'll know what I'm talking about. It was somewhat like that, although hundreds of times louder and constant. It was a very eerie sound and all I could think of was that the walls above us were being pulled apart and ripped out of the house.

The desk where I was sitting would have been on the left of this picture

No sooner had I contemplated what might be causing the groaning and creaking, than it became painfully obvious. My ears started popping like a string of firecrackers being lit off. Pop-pop-pop-pop-pop-pop-pop-pop-pop-pop!

Simultaneously, the duct work from the heating and air conditioning system which we were huddled next to, began imploding. The duct work looked much the same as if you had taken an empty plastic drink bottle and squeezed it or sucked the air out of it.

My worst fears instantly became a reality as the vortex of the tornado moved directly above us. Inside the vortex is very low pressure and outside the vortex is very high pressure. Like a giant vacuum, it sucks things up inside and spits them out. That's why our ears were popping wildly and the air ducts collapsed... because the vortex was sucking everything out of the house above us.

This is the point where I began to get pretty worried. The house was built to withstand a lot of downward pressure from the weight of the structure above it, hence the steel I-beam running the length of the house. But it was never built to withstand the upward pulling force exerted by a tornado directly above. My mind began to race with gruesome images of the house being sucked off the foundation and us with it.

Much to my relief, the vortex slowly moved away from the house, being replaced by the grinding and chunking of the debris pounding down on the floor above us again. We were now on the back side of the vortex. The danger of being in the direct path of the tornado is that you get hit hard twice... once by the front as it approaches and again by the back as it passes.

After the crunching phase passed, it was back to the thunderous locomotive sound which again, was deafeningly loud. The roaring slowly dissipated as the tornado moved away from us.

By this time, I could hear the others in the group, some crying and others desperately voicing their concerns. "Is it over?" "Are we safe now?" "Is our house going to be okay?"

"Yes, everything's going to be fine... we're all okay," I assured them, knowing that we had just survived a head-on encounter with a tornado, and much relieved to still be alive.

I remained hopeful that we might be lucky enough that it wasn't an EF3 or stronger tornado. Even though we had taken a direct hit, the damage from a smaller tornado would be more sustainable.

By the time the tornado passed, we were all covered with debris, mud, and sludge. If you've never been in a tornado, it's hard to describe the mixture of ground up, powdered, and liquified bits of just about everything that lies in the path of the tornado.

Whether it's parts of buildings, appliances, electronics, asphalt, chemicals, auto parts, motor oil, antifreeze, insulation, wood, dirt, trees, etc., it ends up in the debris. The debris gets on and embedded into virtually everything. When mixed with rain it becomes a nasty, greasy, gritty, stinky, dangerous, toxic sludge.

The pilgrims next door with the garden area behind and to the left

If being covered in debris and sludge wasn't bad enough, rain water began to pool on the basement floor, creating a sludge soup all around us. The house was built with several floor drains, but the rain water was coming in faster than the drains could empty it out. At least for the time being, the worst was behind us and we could all breathe a sigh of relief.

When I began assessing the situation and contemplating our next move, I was struck with another wave of absolute fear and panic. It was the smell of natural gas. Most of our appliances were gas powered and we were in the basement with the majority of them.

This can't be happening, I thought, *we just survived a direct hit by a tornado and now we might die in a gas fire or explosion!* *I've got to get out of here and get the main gas valve shut off!*

"What's wrong Tim, where are you going?" Stacey asked, when I began moving away from the group.

"It's the gas... we've got a gas leak," I said, making my way to the workshop area next to us, "and I need to get it shut off now!"

I fumbled through my tool drawers until I located a large adjustable wrench I could use to shut off the gas valve. I grabbed a flashlight out of another drawer and made my way to the stairs.

The stairs were full of debris and lots of pieces of plaster, both big and small, that had fallen from the walls and ceiling. I tripped and fell a few times as I was making my way to the top of the stairs, kicking debris and chunks of plaster everywhere.

Arriving at the top of the stairs sent new waves of panic over me. The door had closed during the tornado and there was a large 2x4 board that had shot between the walls of the stairwell near the top of the door. It was wedged tightly between the studs.

If that wasn't bad enough, a big piece of metal rebar (used to reinforce concrete) had been driven through the wall at the bottom of the door. I pulled on the door and it opened a couple of inches, but not even enough to get my arm through.

The ceiling above me was still relatively intact with all the lath boards and much of the plaster still attached. For all intents and purposes, we were trapped inside our basement with a gas leak!

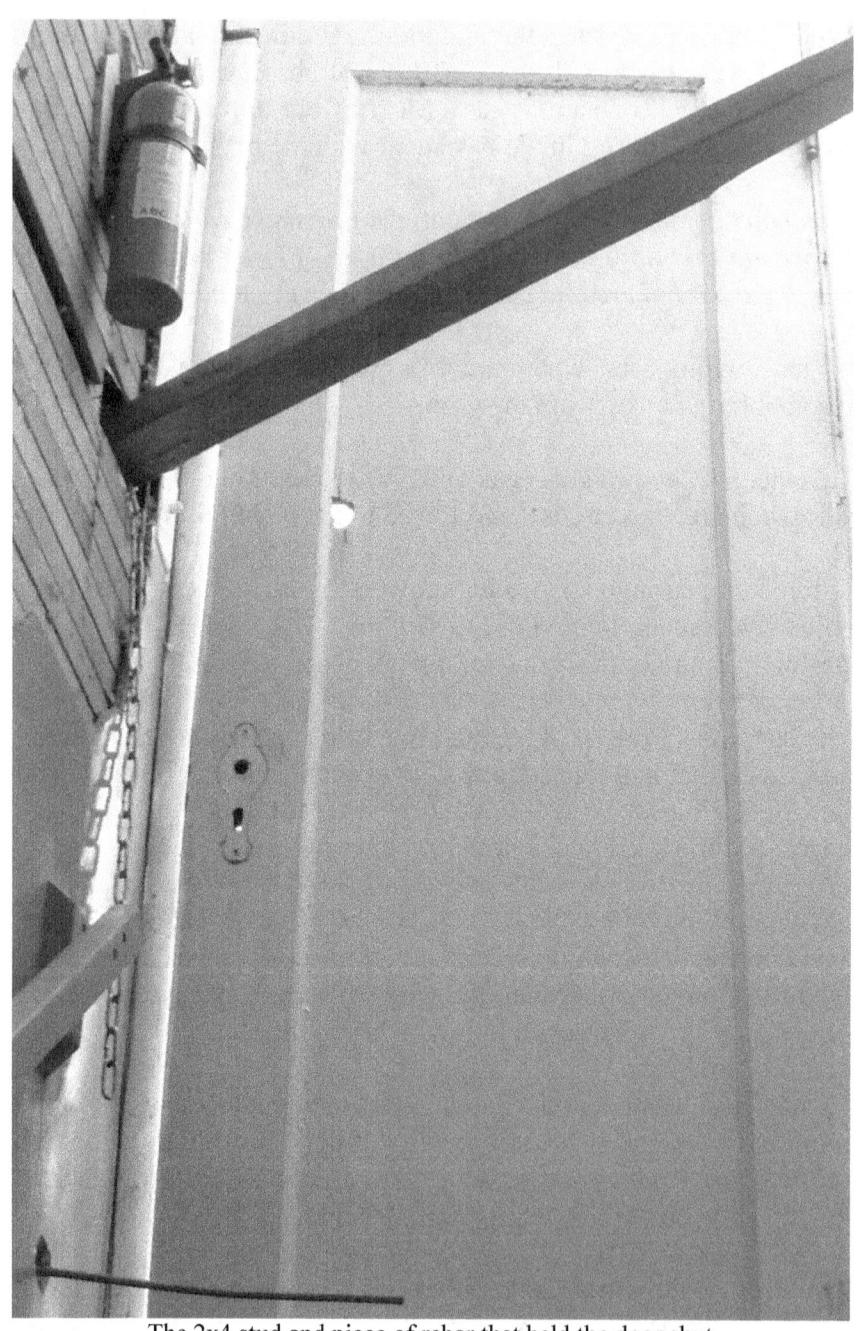

The 2x4 stud and piece of rebar that held the door shut
(more color photos, stories & information available at www.jthoh.com)

Chapter 2

I grabbed the 2x4 that was wedged between the walls and began pushing and pulling, trying to break it loose from the walls, but it was stuck tight. I banged into it with my shoulder and got underneath it, pushing and pulling some more.

I worked at it for what seemed to be an eternity, but was finally able to get it free and pushed it through the wall into the dining room. I then tried to push the rebar back through the kitchen wall. It wasn't going anywhere, so I grabbed ahold of it and pulling it up, bent it at a ninety-degree angle, moving it out of the way just far enough to get the door open.

I opened the door, stepping into the kitchen and was hit with a torrent of rain, drenching me from head to toe. The kitchen walls on the north and west sides of the house were gone. The roof was completely gone. There was nothing to impede the rain as it poured down upon me and the interior of the house.

The winds were starting to diminish, but the rain was coming in buckets. The only way to describe it would be to go to one of those big water parks. Find the place where they have water gushing from a large pipe and put your face in it. That's what it was like standing in the kitchen at the top of the stairs.

The rain was pouring down so hard and there was so much of it that I couldn't see well enough to make out any shapes, much less identify any objects. I could see blotches of colors here and there, but nothing more. I knew where I was in the kitchen and could orient myself enough to find where the back door used to be, and ultimately the stairs that would take me down to ground level.

The gas stove was blocking my path, being held to the wall, still attached by the flex pipe. The hissing of the leaking gas seemed to mock me as I struggled to get past the stove. Fortunately, it was not in the basement with my family, in an enclosed area. At least the gas leaking from the stove was dissipating into the air and rain.

The gas stove (on right) was hissing with a gas leak - notice the hole above the stove where a 2x4 went through the wall, pinning the stairwell door shut

There were piles of boards, bricks, and sheet metal from who knows where, strewn all around. There were parts of walls and miscellaneous building materials that were mixed in with the other piles of appliances and other debris. I felt like a blind person in a forest, trying to maneuver my way to the back of the house.

Once I reached the back steps, it was even worse. The rain let up for a few seconds and I could see parts of other peoples' houses, buildings, cars, trees, and appliances all over the yard. There were downed power poles with electrical lines laying everywhere.

Don't step on any power lines, I kept telling myself as I made my way from the back of the house to the side where the gas meter was located. Along the way, I stepped on nail after rusty nail. One went into my foot so deep that it stuck. I had to stand on the board with my other foot next to it, so I could pull it up and off the nail.

I finally made my way to the gas meter, but I couldn't see well enough through the rain to find the actual valve. I stood there for a couple of minutes before the rain let up enough where I could find the valve and turn it to the closed and off position.

Gas meter at bottom/left of this picture below dining room & kitchen on right

At least the house, or what's left of it didn't blow up, I thought. *I've got to get everyone out of the basement and up to safety.*

I could see a little better by now and avoided most of the rusty nails going back the way I had come. There was no way to avoid all the nails, because the boards of what used to be houses were everywhere, full of nails. When I got back to the door at the top of the stairs, the rain had suddenly died to a sprinkle and I paused to get a look at the neighborhood.

I had never seen such a view of carnage in my life. Not even the old war movies of World War II or any other war movie I've ever seen depicted an image like what I beheld at that very moment. As far as the eye could see, it was a total waste land.

There was an eerie calm and total silence as the sun began to peek through the storm clouds. The sky was no longer green, just dark, gray, and gloomy. Apparently Michelle was right after all... when the sky had turned green, a tornado immediately followed.

How do I prepare my family for what they are about to see, I wondered, *what should I tell them?*

Entire roof, north and east walls blown away

Standing there trying to sort things out in my head, I could hear Stacey desperately calling my name from the basement.

"I'm okay," I yelled, "I got the gas turned off."

When I reached the bottom of the stairs I found my family very concerned, worried, and full of anxiety, not knowing what awaited them beyond the door at the top of the stairs.

"Think of the worst destruction you've ever seen," I said, "whether it's a war movie or something on the news. Now try to imagine that scene of destruction being ten times worse. That's what you're going to see when you walk through that door."

One by one, each member of the family made their way to the top of the stairs, out into the kitchen area. Tears began to flow freely as they surveyed not only our home, but those of our neighbors that surrounded us.

Looking around, it was obvious that it had been raining cars and trucks in the neighborhood. There were vehicles everywhere and the only logical explanation was that they had fallen from the sky. Some were wrapped around trees and power poles.

It was raining cars and trucks in our neighborhood

We noticed our Kia Rondo (seven passenger vehicle) was missing from the driveway at the back of the house. The other vehicles, including our RV, were still somewhere in the neighborhood but there was no sign of the Rondo.

Although we found our other vehicles, none of them were operable. Even if they had been operable, there was no clear path to the streets which were piled high with all kinds of debris as well.

While we stood there, each of us in some varying degree of shock, the scene around us began to turn surreal. Many of the homes nearby had been flattened to the ground, or close to it. Those that hadn't been completely flattened were mostly piles of timbers, bricks, and debris of every kind.

What happened next was like watching ants coming out of their anthill after a rainstorm. We could see an arm here and a leg there, hands pushing boards out of the way, as people slowly emerged from the piles of rubble that were once their homes.

It was like being in a cheesy, B-grade zombie movie as these same people raised themselves out of the piles of rubble, stumbling into the streets, dazed and confused, covered in tornado sludge, and some with blood.

Stacey's NHS sweatshirt - one of the few articles of clothing that survived

I watched a neighbor couple emerge from their destroyed home, carrying their loyal and faithful dog who was badly injured. It's difficult to describe the sadness, pain, and grief on their faces.

They walked past our house and seconds later a single gun shot rang out, underscoring their personal tragedy. Their dog was injured so badly, they had no choice but to put her down.

A similar scene of destruction was everywhere we looked

Where are Max and Jaxon, I wondered, after hearing the gunshot and knowing that our neighbor's pet had just been put down.

Looking around I could see that Heather still had Jaxon in her arms.

"Stacey," I called to my wife, "where's Max?"

I could see tears welling up in her eyes as she approached me.

"She never made it downstairs... I'm so sorry."

"But you told me someone had her," I stammered.

"I knew you would go back up for her, so I had to lie to you to keep you safe."

I could feel the tears running down my cheeks as I imagined my little buddy being violently battered in the tornado and suffering a horrible death. I was grief stricken. Not like I would be if I lost a family member, but very close to that. In my eyes, our pets are part of the family and I am very attached to them, much as if they were my own children.

"Maybe she found some shelter," Stacey said, trying to give me hope, "maybe we'll find her if we look around."

Behind our house where the seven passenger Rondo was parked

Perhaps Stacey was right... maybe Max was alive and maybe she was hiding under some debris. I called out her name repeatedly, walking through the house and around the property, searching through the piles of debris that lay everywhere.

While I was looking for her, the scene quickly changed from one of surreal to something you might see in a war movie. Fires began to pop up here and there and we could see the smoke and flames flickering against the dimly lit skyline.

And then, almost as if synchronized, emergency vehicle sirens began to shatter the eerie silence. The post-apocalyptic darkness was lit up by the flashing lights of every imaginable emergency vehicle. The sound of helicopters and their flashing lights showed their presence in the sky. Before long, there were military vehicles driving through the streets.

There were emergency vehicles from all over the area and all over the country. I have never seen so many emergency vehicles in one place like I witnessed that night. It wasn't long before the orchestra of sirens became so loud they nearly overshadowed the roar of the tornado that had just passed.

First responders, neighbors, and good samaritans were everywhere, helping people, digging through the rubble, looking for people who might be trapped.

There were many stray animals wandering around as if they had no place to go or didn't know how to get there. *Maybe Max is out there lost somewhere,* I hoped, *and maybe someone will find her and take her to the animal shelter so I can get her later.*

Turning my focus back to my family, I knew that we needed to find a safe place to get out of the elements. Some of the neighbors said there were more tornado warnings and more rain on the way. I wasn't about to keep us in harm's way any longer. We had to find some safety... somehow... somewhere.

I pulled my cell phone out of my dripping wet pants pocket, but it was not working. Stacey and the girls each had a cell phone, but couldn't place any calls. The only thing that worked was incoming texts. Fortunately for us, the pilgrims' cell phone could still get a connection for both outbound and inbound texts.

"Do you think your parents would mind if we stayed with them," I asked Stacey.

"I'm sure they won't mind," she said, "they'd probably like it."

"Tiffany, can we borrow your cell phone," I asked, "to text Grandma and Grandpa to see if they can come and get us?"

"Sure thing," Tiffany replied, handing her cell phone to Stacey.

Stacey started tapping on the phone; *tornado. house gone. everyone ok. can't call. cars gone. call tim to come get us. stacey.* When she was finished, she hit the SEND key.

Stacey received a text message from her father, *we are on our way.*

Looking south down Joplin Ave. in front of our house

Meanwhile, about seventy miles to the south of us in Bentonville, Arkansas, my brother-in-law, Tim, and his wife, Aly, were enjoying a leisurely evening at church. They were attending the graduation ceremony of their daughter, Ashley, from seminary class.

They were joined by their friends, Jim and Sharon. As the other attendees were finding their seats, Jim leaned over, pointing to his cell phone which displayed a weather radar map of the area.

"Look at that crazy, nasty storm that's north of us," he said.

"I'm sure glad that we're down here," Tim replied, studying the numerous dark red areas on the radar image, "I wouldn't want to be up there in that mess."

"It's far enough away that it shouldn't affect the graduation," Jim said, stuffing the phone into his pocket.

After the ceremony commenced, Tim's phone began vibrating, indicating an incoming call. It was from his father, Glenn. He ignored the call thinking it probably wasn't anything significant and figured he'd return the call after the festivities had ended.

The phone buzzed again, but since a message hadn't been left the first time, he ignored it a second time. On the third call with no message, he texted his father and asked him to please leave a message, so he might know if it was important enough to disrupt the ceremony.

On the fourth call, a voice message was left. During a musical number, Tim leaned down to listen to the message. It was his father's voice, and he was clearly distraught and sounded panicked.

"Tim," he said, as serious as he'd ever heard him, "your sister just texted me and their house has been hit by a tornado and we need to go get them!"

He leaned over and whispering in his wife's ear, told her what he had just heard. Jumping out of their seats to leave, Jim was right on their heels.

Hurrying outside the church building he relayed his father's voice message to Jim. Tim was somewhat in shock as his mind raced with images of news footage of other tornado damage he had seen over the years.

Tornadoes in this part of the country are usually devastating, he thought, fighting back the tears and trying to remain strong and focused on the task at hand.

Looking at the back of our house from the pilgrims' back driveway

"Aly, do you want to come with me to get Stacey and her family?"

"No," Jim interrupted, "she should stay here. I'll go with you. Let's hurry up there and bring them back. Aly, let Sharon know what's going on and tell her I'll be back as soon as possible."

No amount of gratitude could have been adequately expressed at that moment to a friend and brother so eager and willing to serve. Through his tears, all Tim could muster up was a simple, "thank you!" From that moment, he began to pray in his heart for guidance and for the safety of his sister and her family.

Glenn had recently received a liver transplant and was under strict doctor's orders to avoid all traveling. However, at that moment it would have taken a full battalion of heavily armed soldiers to restrain him and his wife, Dianne, from helping one of their children during such a crisis.

Parts of other people's houses had blown in all around our house

Tim, his parents, and Jim met at a local gas station to fill up before continuing, anticipating that there would be neither power nor open gas stations once they arrived in Joplin. While they were fueling their vehicles, tornado sirens began blaring all around them.

What if a tornado hits Bentonville or Rogers when we're gone, Tim thought, trying to force a feeling of dread out of his mind. As he contemplated this dilemma, a peaceful feeling came over him and he felt a spiritual assurance that everything at home would be fine. The others felt the same way, that they should proceed northward to get their family.

Abby's bedroom from the outside looking in

Tim headed up the caravan. Jim was right behind him with Glenn and Dianne bringing up the rear. They kept in contact with each other as best they could via cell phones.

At times it was nearly impossible to hear over the wind, rain, and hail that assaulted them violently and relentlessly, coming at them horizontally, blowing them all over the road. They felt like they were in a giant blender, being beaten and tossed around at the will of mother nature, as she randomly hit the PULSE button.

The rescue team was doing their best to drive as fast as possible, but visibility was not much more than about ten yards, which impeded their progress tremendously. The elements were in such commotion all around them that Tim half expected to see a cow fly across the road at any moment.

They hadn't traveled northward more than twenty miles when the hail and rain were pounding down so relentlessly they felt it best to pull over, hoping that it might let up enough to make for safe traveling once again. Much to their dismay, they continued to be battered by the elements as they waited on the side of the road.

Tim's parents lost cell phone service and he was unable to advise them to pull over to the side of the road. In the horrible conditions, his parents couldn't see well enough to make out the vehicles on the side of the road and ended up driving past him.

As our little band of refugees waited for the rescue party, we made our way around the neighborhood to check on friends and neighbors. Much to our relief, everyone around us had survived. There were a few who had bumps, bruises, scrapes, and minor cuts, but nothing major or life-threatening (with the exception of the neighbor's dog being put down).

One couple told us how they had taken shelter in the hall closet to ride out the storm. When they entered the closet, the door was facing south, but when they opened the door after the tornado had passed, the door was facing west.

I looked at their pile of rubble and miraculously, the only thing in the house still standing was that very closet where they survived. *How*, I wondered, *did that closet turn ninety degrees and remain standing while the rest of the house was ripped to shreds?*

Another house laid in ruins across the street from us. It had a floor plan and a garage in the basement similar to ours. The tornado had blown down the garage door and the winds ripped through the basement, lifting the house off its foundation, turning it inside out and upside down before dropping it back into the basement.

Inside Heather's bedroom looking south where the pilgrims' house used to be

How lucky and blessed we were, I thought, knowing that something similar to that, by all reason, should have happened to our house. It's not like the two houses were on opposite sides of town... they probably weren't more than thirty or forty yards apart.

When the tornado had passed over our house, a strange thing happened. Everything in the center of the bedrooms (the bedrooms were on the south side) was sucked up and out of the rooms, while most of the things that were in or near the corners remained.

The beds were sucked out of the center of the rooms, but the night stands and dressers stayed inside. As a result, we were able to find our wallets in the dresser. We were very fortunate that, at the very least, we had our driver's licenses, credit cards, and bank cards.

As I stood there pondering our good fortune and blessings, a teen-aged boy, Chris, who was a friend of the family, came walking down the street, stopping at our place.

"What in the world are you doing here," I asked, very much surprised to see him.

"When the tornado hit," he said matter-of-factly, "I had to make sure you were all okay."

"Did you walk over here or did someone drop you off?"

"I walked. I'm going to stay here with you until my parents can get here. I already talked to them, and you can stay at our house."

"Well, that's mighty nice of you Chris, but Stacey's family is headed to town right now and we'll be staying with them. But, when your folks get here tell them we really appreciate the offer."

What a great kid, I thought, *making arrangements for our family to stay with his, and walking all this way to persuade us to go with him.* The fact that we have a teenage daughter may have had something to do with it, but nonetheless, a great kid!

I gathered the family around and we walked across the street to the parking lot of the Salvation Army thrift store. We stopped in the middle of the parking lot and turned around to look back at what had once been our homes... ours and the pilgrims' next door.

"I'm going to miss that house," I said, reaching my arm around Stacey, pulling her close, feeling a lump welling up in my throat, "it's the house that saved our family."

Inside the living room looking over the porch

She laid her head on my shoulder and I could feel her body gently shaking as she began sniffling. With tears running down her face, she looked up at me, her eyes full of sadness, her bottom lip turned down and quivering.

"I love our house," she said, the pain evident in her voice, "we put

44

so much of our life into it and now it's gone!"

"It's okay Baby, we can rebuild the house, better than before."

"It will never be the same again... nothing will ever be the same."

I tried to reassure her that everything was going to get better... some how... some way... at some time in the future... but *when*, was anybody's guess.

The streets began filling with other refugees who were carrying bags, personal belongings, children, or pets in their arms, walking in different directions. Where they were all headed, I didn't know, but everyone seemed to know that they needed to get out of there, to a drier, safer place.

When we headed down Main Street away from the devastation, Chris joined us and was determined that we were going to stay with him and his family. Short of hog tying me and carrying me on a pole to his house, he did everything in his power to get us to go with him. Did I say what a great kid he is?

Many miles to the south of us, Tim and Jim waited alongside the now deserted highway, hoping the weather would break. Jim had contacted a friend to get an update on the weather situation.

Their friend, Brendan, was looking at a radar image online and told him that they needed to move on quickly, as there were tornado cells directly above them!

Jim quickly phoned Tim.

"We've got to get out of here now," he said insistently, "I just talked to Brendan and there are tornado cells right over our heads!"

They quickly pulled their vehicles back onto the road and kept them pointed northward, being pummeled relentlessly by the elements every inch of the way.

Unable to contact the other members of the rescue party, Glenn and Dianne had exited the highway just a few miles further, taking shelter at a local gas station / convenience store near Anderson.

They hurried inside where they were greeted by some firemen who were advising everyone in the store to find a safe place to ride out the storm, insistent that they remain inside.

Looking through the living room and Heather's bedroom

Dianne finally got a cell phone signal and called to see where the others were. Tim and Jim had gotten beyond the storm cell, along with all the rain and hail, several miles beyond Anderson.

Knowing that things were going to be clearer ahead, Glenn and Dianne decided to get back on the road. When they began making their way toward the door, one of the firemen stretched his arms out towards them with the palms of his hands forward and advised them to stay put.

"Can you force us to stay," Dianne inquired.

"No, we can't force you to stay, but I would strongly recommend it for your own safety."

"We're leaving then. My daughter and her family lost everything in the Joplin tornado and we need to get there as soon as we can."

They walked out the door, into the pounding rain and hail. Climbing into their vehicle, they drove slowly into the darkness, risking their own safety to resume the rescue mission.

Except for the faint orange glow of fires burning and the twinkling lights emanating from emergency vehicles and helicopters off in the distance, Joplin lay in total darkness when Tim and Jim arrived at the outer city limits.

Tim's heart sank into his stomach as he passed car after car that had been blown off the road, one wrapped around a tree, another flipped over in a field by the highway. There were eighteen-wheeler trucks turned over up and down the median of the highway. Trying to take it all in, he could make out a few remnants of where a gas station once stood before it had been blown off the landscape.

The first exit they came to was barricaded. They proceeded to the next exit where they were able to make their way over to the north side of town. There they found what looked to be a main road that they hoped would lead them to where they needed to be.

Unfortunately, after traveling only a short distance down the road they were stopped by police, who had closed the road for emergency vehicles only. Tim pleaded with the officer to let him through so he could get to his family. The officer denied his request and told him they would need to find another way.

They turned around, drove back about a half mile, pulled over and stopped. Jim piled into Tim's pickup truck and together they reviewed their map. They saw another route that might get them into the downtown area. They drove over a few blocks, made a turn and proceeded southward.

Houses, sheds, and trees near the pilgrims' house, as seen from the alley

Driving through the thick darkness, they witnessed the most solemn, horrific sights in their headlights. Power poles and electrical lines that had been knocked down were laying all over the ground. Building materials, trees, and bushes were scattered everywhere they looked. The smell of natural gas permeated the air. Any people they saw on the streets were walking around in a zombielike daze. Tim asked a man walking in the street if he knew how to get to Main Street from where they were.

"I think it's over that way," the man answered, pointing down a street full of debris, littered with battered and mangled cars. They continued down the road, swerving back and forth around the cars, power poles, trees, and debris.

Houses, sheds, and trees, including the neighboring houses are all gone

Ahead in the distance they could see a circle of lights. Proceeding further, they could see some cars that were parked around a collapsed apartment building with their headlights shining in on the imploded wreckage.

Driving slowly by, they saw people frantically digging, throwing boards aside, screaming for their family, friends, and neighbors. Tim's heart ached and went out to all those people struggling to rescue loved ones, but feeling a greater sense of urgency to find his sister and her family, they kept moving.

They continued to inch their way down the streets, having to backtrack and take many alternate routes because so many streets were impassable. He began to wonder if they would ever make it through the carnage and reach his family. After what seemed like an eternity of going one block forward and two blocks back, his phone began to ring.

The kitchen table and entire fireplace near the street

Further down Main Street, our group had taken temporary shelter under a covered sidewalk at a strip mall. I called Tim to give him an update on our circumstances and ascertain his location.

Having gotten off the main roads and not knowing how best to proceed, he was anxious for me to direct him through the back streets to where we were now waiting.

"Tell me what stores, buildings or landmarks you see around you so I can get an idea of exactly where you are right now."

Looking around him through the darkness, all he could say was, "it's gone, it's all gone... there's nothing here."

"What street signs do you see?"

"None, there aren't any. The buildings, the trees, the power poles, the signs... they're all gone. Everything is flattened and strewn everywhere, there are no lights anywhere... just total darkness. I can't see much of anything and I don't know if we're going to be able to drive any further than we are right now."

"Let me make some calls and see if there's any way we can make it to where you are. Just sit tight and we'll call you when we have something figured out."

Realizing the roads were more or less impassable, they decided to double back to the north side of Joplin and wait at the Target parking lot. There they could wait for another call and figure out their next move.

While they waited in the parking lot they watched countless ambulances coming and going, racing in every direction. They felt helpless and full of despair as they sat there, waiting for a call.

After what felt like forever, Stacey called her brother to give him an update. The pilgrims had been in contact with some friends, Jason and Laila who lived nearby, but out of the path of the tornado. They made arrangements for the pilgrims to stay with them. They were also gracious enough to offer to take us down the road to Diamond in order for us to meet up with Stacey's family.

Before we left Joplin, we made sure that Chris would be safely retrieved by his parents. We were very grateful to him and his parents for offering to let our family stay with them.

Driving to meet us, Tim called his parents to let them know that he and Jim would be meeting up with us. He assured them that everyone was okay and the best thing for them to do was to turn around, go back home and wait for everyone to get there.

Our house after a snow storm, just months before the tornado struck

When we rendezvoused with our rescue party in Diamond, Stacey, the girls, and I each had a plastic garbage bag with what little clothes and belongings remained that we could grab. We were all dirty, wet, distraught, and exhausted.

Tim said he would never forget the feeling of gratitude and love he had for his Heavenly Father for bringing us to safety. He walked up to his sister and hugged her with all his might. Crying together, all he could say to her was, "it's okay, you're safe now."

The journey to Arkansas was a very emotional ride for us. We had just been snatched from the jaws of death of one tornado and now there were more tornado watches and warnings all around us and throughout the state of Arkansas.

Our anxiety levels rose as we listened to our rescuers recount their story of being nearly swept off the road as they made their way to rescue us. Now we would have to drive back through the storm cells that continued to develop all around us.

How can you relax after just surviving a tornado when your new, temporary residence has tornado sirens going off and more warnings and watches in effect? What really worried us is that my in-law's place didn't have a basement or any kind of storm shelter. If a tornado did come our way, we would have nowhere to run... nowhere to hide!

By the time our little band of refugees and our rescuers had made it safely to my in-laws place, more than eight hours had passed since the tornado hit us.

We were still wet and filthy from head to toe. We were worn out, not just physically, but mentally and emotionally as well. I began to understand very intimately, the meaning of the phrase, "rode hard and put away wet!"

Grace sitting on the front steps of what was once her home

The built-in china hutch virtually unscathed, part of the chimney in front
(more color photos, stories & information available at www.jthoh.com)

Chapter 3

Just when I thought it couldn't possibly get any worse, it did. I have a really messed up back and neck, resulting from three high speed rear-end collisions in the past. At home I had always slept in my Tempur-pedic bed, but the bed in the spare room was horrible. I think the bed was once used as a medieval torture device.

The following morning I was ready to confess to being the third gunman on the grassy knoll who shot JFK. I felt like the hunchback of Notre Dame... I couldn't stand erect, my back hurt so much. Needless to say, before the end of that day, I was going to purchase a memory foam mattress to help my aching back.

Once I was able to get all the kinks out of my back, I knew that we had better get on the phone quickly and start making calls to the insurance companies to get some claims started. The first call we needed to make was to the auto insurance company. Since all of our vehicles had been totaled, we needed to secure a rental car. Unfortunately for us, the Rondo was the only vehicle that had full coverage, while the others only had liability coverage.

When I got someone on the phone, I explained that our vehicles had been destroyed in the tornado. The woman I spoke to told me that the only one they could help us with was the Rondo. I agreed with her and told her that we needed to get a rental car ASAP so we could bet back to Joplin and gather our personal belongings.

What happened next was somewhat bizarre. She asked me what amount of damage the Rondo had sustained. I told her that I didn't really know because the car was missing after the tornado had blown through. She began to quiz me as if to suggest that I was simply hiding the vehicle and trying to get another one with the insurance proceeds.

"We will have to see the vehicle and inspect it before we can pay out on any claim," she assured me.

"That's great, tell your agent to let me know if he finds it. I'd like to know how far it went from our house."

Our beautiful and fragrant magnolia tree

The homeowner's insurance company went a little better, but not much. When I reached them, I told the woman that I needed to make a claim on the house, because it had been destroyed by the tornado. She asked me what amount of damage was sustained. I told her there were a few walls still standing but most were not and the roof was gone, along with most of the contents. I was shocked when she said, "you probably should get some tarps and cover the damaged areas."

The magnolia tree, no longer beautiful or fragrant... just more debris

Because I was anxious to end the call, I didn't ask the question that I really wanted to ask her, "do they make house sized tarps, and if so, where can I buy one?"

Not surprising, it took several hours before we could get a rental car because the rental companies were out of vehicles for many miles in every direction around the Joplin area. We finally got a car by early afternoon and were on our way back to the house.

When we pulled into town, the skies were solid gray and it was raining steadily. The forecast called for more rain, severe thunderstorm warnings, and a tornado watch.

That's just all we need, I thought, *talk about getting kicked in the gut when you're already down*!

House across the street that was picked up and crushed into the basement

When we pulled the rental car up to the house, our hearts sank and our spirits quickly deflated. It was painful to look at the broken shell of our once beautiful home that we had poured so much of our lives into. Anything that had not have been destroyed by the tornado was quickly being ruined by the constant deluge of rain.

There wasn't much we could do as far as digging for any personal items or belongings because of the rain and overall dangerous conditions of the surroundings. However, I wanted to walk around the house again to see if I could find Max. I walked all around the house, calling her name and looking through the debris, but still no sign of her. It just made the already bad day that much worse as I began to lose hope of ever finding her alive.

Across the street I noticed a couple of the neighbors, Aaron and Ashley, who were digging through a pile of boards, appliances, and other rubble that was once their home. They weren't home when the tornado hit, but their four dogs were. It took them a lot of digging, but they finally rescued all of them alive.

Looking up from her digging, I made eye contact with Ashley and waved to her. Her countenance quickly changed from distress and sorrow to happiness and excitement. Dropping what was in her hands, she came running across the street waving her hands.

"We found Max," she yelled excitedly, "we have Max!"

My spirits soared as I raced over to meet her. She explained how they had been walking around the neighborhood and when they passed by our house they heard some whimpering. They went into the bathroom and there, under a pile of sheet metal, bricks, boards, and other debris they found her in the bathtub.

I was elated to hear the news.

"Where is she?" I asked, anxious to reunite with my little buddy.

"My sister is keeping her... she's on her way here now."

It wasn't long before Ashley's sister, Cara, pulled up in the street. Stepping out of her car, she hurried over to us and gave me a quick run down of Max's condition. She was banged up a bit and scared, but she had not sustained any serious injuries.

"She's at my house, so you'll have to drive a few miles out of your way to get her."

"I'd drive to Texas to get her!"

We thanked Aaron and Ashley, jumped in the car and followed Cara to her house where Max was sitting quietly on the living room floor. I scooped my little buddy up into my arms, thanking Cara for taking good care of her, and then headed back to the car.

The bathtub (bottom right) where Max was rescued

For the next ten minutes, Max licked my hand so much I thought she might wear the skin away. I could tell she was very happy to be reunited with her family, and so was I.

We decided to head back to Arkansas since there wasn't much we could do at the house in the pouring rain. On the way back, I made a couple more phone calls to the various utility companies, to get our services suspended.

On every call I had made that day, from the insurance companies to the utility companies, the conversation began much the same way. After I told them where we lived, they responded with how sorry they were that my family and I were *victims* of the tornado.

I was somewhat taken aback by these repeated words. I didn't really see myself or my family members as being *victims* of the tornado. If anything we were *survivors* at best and *refugees* at worst. Even though we had been violently jerked from our home, we were still alive and moving forward, albeit painfully slow.

Meanwhile, about one hundred fifty miles to the north in Kansas City, Sloane was preparing for her next assignment. She was a news reporter for a local TV station. She would be traveling to Joplin the next day to cover stories of the tornado and its aftermath. When she was leaving the studio for the day, she grabbed her cell phone, dialed it and placed it to her ear.

"Hey Dan," she said into the phone, "we're going to Joplin... will you be ready to leave in the morning?"

Dan, her husband and a professional photographer, had already been gathering his gear together, preparing to make the trip. Even if his wife hadn't received an assignment, he had planned to make the journey himself. He wanted to photograph the tragedy from a more humanistic and less journalistic angle.

"I'm packing my equipment now," he said, "we should be able to leave first thing in the morning, if you want."

"That's perfect. I'm just leaving the studio, so I'll see you in a little while."

Dan ended the call, pressing his cell phone into his pocket as he continued gathering his photographic equipment and other things he would need for the trip.

The following morning, they hurriedly loaded their things into their car and sped out of the driveway. They needed to leave early in order to beat the traffic that was starting to build.

Stacey and I were on our way to Joplin, stopping first at a gas station / convenience store. We needed to get some gas and I wanted to fuel myself up with a breakfast croissant sandwich.

The woman running the cash register asked how our day was. We told her about our experience and what do you know, she used the "V" word. It seemed like we were going to be *victims*, whether we liked it or not.

Our RV (center), Irving Elementary (left), power substation (right)

Driving back to Joplin, I thought a lot about the whole *victim* thing and it didn't sit well with me. In my mind, I felt that if I bought into being a *victim*, then I might also feel that I was entitled to something... that others *owed* me something, just because I was unfortunate enough to have been in the path of the tornado. To me, *victim* was a negative label, while *survivor* or *refugee* was much more positive and even more applicable.

I was raised in a very modest home and have always had the attitude that, *if it's yours to do and you've got to do it, you might as well try to make the best of a bad situation.* That's how I was feeling going into the whole cleanup and recovery aspect of the post tornado efforts.

Meanwhile, about seventy miles to the north of us, Dan and Sloane were just pulling into Joplin, meeting up with her camera crew. She grabbed some of her things and loaded them into the news vehicle. She kissed Dan and wished him a good day, promising to call him later to see how things were going.

As she and the camera crew began driving into the swath of destruction, they were overwhelmed with what they saw everywhere they looked. They pulled the car to a stop and Sloane jumped out of the car, her mind swimming, trying to take it all in and put it into some sort of perspective.

Her entire body began shaking uncontrollably as a flood of emotions poured over her. She had never been so overwhelmed with sadness and shock. She couldn't understand how a tornado could decimate a town so completely as this one had.

It's like a war zone, she thought as she watched an elderly couple emerging from the remnants of their home that was now nothing more than a hovel. Visiting briefly, they invited her inside. She followed them to the tiny bathroom that had saved their lives, listening intently as they recounted their harrowing experience.

Several blocks away, Dan steered his car slowly through the streets littered with debris. He was in complete shock and disbelief that what he was seeing had really happened. Everywhere he looked he saw a scene that seemed unreal.

He sank into deep despair and anxiety for the people who had been affected. His heart truly ached for people he had never met, in a way that he'd never felt before.

He had provided photographic coverage for various news and journalistic stories before and seen much destruction on TV news reports. But, to see it firsthand and witness the raw power and intensity of this storm was something that he hadn't expected and for which he wasn't fully prepared.

The sheer magnitude of destruction was dizzying and he was finding it difficult to determine a starting point. How could he possibly capture the enormity of this disaster while focusing on the personal tragedies of the survivors he hoped to photograph?

I spray painted my first message on Heather's bedroom wall

With his camera slung around his neck, he continued slowly down one street after another. In his mind, he tried to create a visual image that would somehow develop into a linear story rather than one catastrophe literally piled on top of another.

He knew the photos he would shoot on this trip would be unlike any he had ever taken before. The real story wasn't about the rampage of the tornado, but rather the physical, mental, emotional, and spiritual struggle of those who had been beaten down so profoundly, who were now trying to make it through another day.

He wondered how he could adequately capture the emotions that percolated everywhere he turned, through his camera's lens. How could he effectively tell the story through pictures, while at the same time being compassionate and sensitive to those people who had been through so much and now had so little?

By the time Stacey and I reached the house, I had decided that I didn't want to accept the idea of being a victim. Instead, I wanted to inspire the neighbors and perhaps others who might drive by. With resolute determination, I went into the basement to what was left of my work area and grabbed a can of black spray paint.

Returning topside, I went to what had been Heather's bedroom and climbed on a pile of debris and broken furniture. I shook the spray paint and proceeded to write "GOD BLESS JOPLIN!" on the neon green wall.

I then proceeded to the living room, climbed on a pile of broken furniture and collapsed walls and wrote, "DOWN, NOT OUT!!" on the yellow wall, above the arched walkway between the living room and dining room.

I hoped that anyone who saw our house would know that we were not only positive and hopeful, but that we acknowledged the presence of a supreme power greater than ourselves who had blessed our community greatly. There was no doubt in my mind that God really had blessed Joplin and its residents, in spite of all the destruction left in the wake of the tornado!

I had hoped that my messages might inspire others in our community. My hope was that rather than feeling depressed and hopeless, they might feel more positive, have hope, and get on with what needed to be done.

My second message was spray painted on the living room wall

With my inspirational messages now prominently displayed on the wreckage of our home, I went back to the business at hand. The first thing we wanted to do was dig through the rubble, hoping to find some personal memorabilia that could be saved.

While I was traversing my way through the obstacle course that our house had become, I noticed a news crew that had pulled up in the Salvation Army parking lot across the street. A man got out of the news van, walked across the street and onto the concrete slab that had been our front porch.

"I noticed the messages on your walls," he said, "and wondered if we might be able to talk to you."

I climbed over a large pile of debris and worked my way over to greet him.

"You'll have to excuse the mess, we hadn't planned on having company today, otherwise we would have cleaned up a bit."

He smiled and asked a few questions about our experience in the tornado. He then asked if Stacey and I would mind talking to him and the film crew. I went and got Stacey from the back bedroom where she was working.

He wanted to know how our spirits could be so positive in spite of what we had just been through. We explained that we were blessed to still be alive and together as a family. That we would just have to take it one day at a time, until enough days had passed and we were able to get beyond it.

After the interview it was back to work. Standing there, looking at the chaos and destruction, it was daunting. I tried to visualize a plan, but it was overwhelming. Where do you start when there's so much that needs to be done?

I decided to start cleaning in our bedroom. The book that Stacey had just finished was stored electronically on the tower computer in our bedroom. The computer was trashed and had been sitting in the rubble through about twelve inches of rain.

Still, I had hope... I had copied the book onto a USB drive the day before the tornado. I reasoned that I might be lucky enough to find the "needle in the haystack."

I got a five gallon bucket, a pair of leather gloves, and on my hands and knees, began inching my way through a small mountain of debris. Stacey was well into search and recovery mode, moving from room to room, focusing on photos and other personal items.

Stacey and Aly found an egg in the rubble without so much as a scratch on it

The nature of the tornado seemed very bizarre, almost selective and discriminatory. For example, you could look in some areas of town where all the homes were destroyed, except for a house here and a house there. There was no rhyme or reason as to what was destroyed and what was spared.

So it was in our house. Occasionally, Stacey would find a picture or other item that was completely unscathed, as if it had been set aside and returned after the tornado passed.

Another strange example of this is the broom that Stacey had leaned against the concrete between the back steps and the deck when she had finished sweeping the sand on the bricks.

The steps were made of solid concrete. The handrails were made out of two inch steel pipes, which were set into the concrete steps. The steel handrail closest to the broom had been pulled completely out of the concrete and was nowhere to be found. The other handrail was bent out about a foot. Much of the deck had been destroyed as well. However, the broom did not move an inch. It was in the exact same spot as when Stacey had put it there.

I have pondered the broom not moving... not even an inch, knowing that it weighed only a pound or two. It doesn't make sense to me that it wouldn't have moved during a frenzied tornado.

After much consideration, I've come to the conclusion that it really did move. My theory is that it ended up several miles down the road in some farmer's field. However, because it is a "magical witch's broom," it returned to where its owner had placed it!

I love to share this story with others, but understandably, Stacey isn't a big fan of my theory of the broom's pristine survival.

Stacey took a week off from work so she could rescue as many personal items as possible. Initially, the digging was tough because there was so much heavy debris. Not just bricks and boards, but furniture and appliances... some ours and some of the neighbors' that ended up in our house.

The work was even more difficult with all the rusty nails that we literally couldn't avoid stepping on, along with broken glass, razor sharp pieces of sheet metal, and other busted and broken debris. Plus, there was no way to tell for sure just how structurally sound any remaining parts of the house were.

It wasn't long before I heard a scream from Stacey. I rushed out of the bedroom to find her sitting on a huge chunk of the chimney that had fallen into the dining room. She had one leg crossed over the top of the other, wincing, as she gently and slowly unlaced her shoe, removing it from her foot.

"What happened?"

"I slipped... I think I might have broken my ankle."

"Let me take you to the emergency room!"

"No, the hospitals are all overwhelmed with patients who need to be there more than I do at the moment."

Debris was piled up several feet high throughout the house

"At least go in for an x-ray."

"No, not right now... maybe later. See if you can find that CAM boot for me."

A CAM (Controlled Ankle Motion) boot is used with ankle and foot injuries to limit movement and aid in healing. We just happened to have one.

I'm one of those people who likes to be prepared for any emergency. I don't know if it's the Boy Scout in me or some other force (Stacey calls it *hoarding*), but I had acquired a vast array of medical devices, a CAM boot being one of them.

Some of the smaller medical equipment was kept in the hall closet. I made my way back through the house and down the hall to the closet. Much to my joy, the CAM boot was laying right on top of the rubble. It was wet and covered with sludge, but it was intact with all its pieces.

Stacey quickly fitted it to her foot and strapped it into place. Incredibly, it fit her perfectly. I helped her to her feet and she took a few steps, very gingerly.

"Are you going to be okay with that... is it safe for you to be working around here with that on your foot?"

"I think I'll be alright," she said, hobbling a few more steps, "it's just really sore right now."

I didn't know whether to be more depressed because of her injury or feel blessed because we had the CAM boot in the closet. I decided to go with the feelings of being blessed. I was just hoping that we wouldn't have any more of these *blessings* any time soon!

I was so inspired with Stacey's tenacity that I retrieved my can of spray paint, went to the kitchen and wrote "PRESS ON!" over the arched hood that was above the stove. *Surely*, I surmised, *there will be others with similar injuries who might need a little encouragement.*

We both went back to work, being especially careful of where and how we moved through the house. After Stacey injured her ankle it became apparent that the best way to move between the front and back of the house was to go out to the street or alley and around the house, rather than through the debris piles, risking more injury.

Abby holding Grace and Olivia

It hadn't been long when a car pulled up in the street behind our rental car and a man stepped out. He waved from the street. I waved back and began making my way down to the street to see what he wanted. Shaking my hand, he introduced himself as Dan.

"Nice to meet you Dan. I'm Tim and that's my wife, Stacey, up there digging around like she's an archeologist with a mission."

"I'm a photographer and I was wondering if you would mind if I took some pictures of the two of you with your house. What I'd like to do is more of a portrait, with your house in the background. I'll bring you copies later, if that's okay with you."

"I'm okay with that, but let me see about my wife."

I went to Stacey and explained what Dan was interested in doing. She said she was fine with that, so I took her by the hand, making our way carefully down to the back yard.

By this time, Dan had a camera mounted on a tripod with an umbrella flash next to it. After he connected his equipment, he took a reading with his light meter. He took a practice shot, looked at it, made some adjustments and took another shot.

"I think I'm ready if you are," he said, focusing the camera lens.

I stood close to Stacey, with my arm around her, looking into the camera lens as the flash popped brilliantly in our eyes. He repositioned his camera and took another shot.

"Would you mind if I took some pictures of your house?"

"Not at all, just be careful of all the rusty nails and broken glass."

He walked around the house, shooting additional pictures. When he was finished, he asked what we thought of him going through the neighborhood and taking pictures of other families.

"Do you think people would find it offensive," he asked, "or would they appreciate having a picture to remind them of this time?"

"I don't think they would see it negatively," Stacey said, "at some point, it may mean a lot to them, to show to their grandkids."

"I agree with Stacey," I interjected, "there may be some who don't want to be bothered, but I think what you're doing is a positive thing and I'm glad you stopped by and took our picture."

Stacey (with CAM boot) and I - Photo used with permission:

Dan thanked us as he was loading the equipment into his car. "I'll be back in touch," he said, handing me a business card, "if you don't hear from me in a couple of weeks, contact me."

Stacey and I thanked him. He climbed back in his car, drove down the street and around the corner.

"That was very nice of him to do that," she said, reaching down to pick up a soup spoon off the ground, "I'm really glad he stopped by and we got to meet him."

"Me too. What are you going to do with that," I asked, pointing at the spoon in her hand.

"I'm going to keep it. It's a little dirty, but it'll clean up and still get the soup from the bowl to your mouth."

Stacey was right, if we found something that was still usable, we kept it. It was almost as if the things that survived had earned the right to stay with us.

As the morning wore on, many more people began to fill the streets. Several of them were neighbors who, like us, had come to look for personal belongings in their respective piles of rubble. Many more were emergency responders looking for survivors, utility workers turning off water valves, etc. Others were onlookers who came to view the destruction firsthand. All of these people I expected to see after the tornado had struck.

One thing I didn't expect to see was a man and a woman from St. Mary's church walking down the street. Their church sat on the hill about four blocks to the west of our house on the same street.

Like us, their church was in the direct path of the tornado. Much of the structure of their building had been ripped apart and strewn all over the neighborhood. In fact, one of the steel arch supports from their building had crashed into our kitchen where the cabinets and sink once stood.

It wasn't so much that I was surprised to see them walking through the neighborhood, as much as what they were doing. Even though their church had, for all intents and purposes, been completely destroyed, they were walking through the neighborhood giving money to people whose homes and lives had just been shattered.

St. Mary's Church with steel beams exposed on roof structures

How is that, I wondered, *they're going to have to rebuild their entire church from the ground up and they're here handing out money, that at some point I would think they would need for themselves. They clearly have the faith that God will bless them for helping the least of these their brethren, and provide for them later when they need help.*

It turned out that this would not be an isolated incident as there were others who came through the neighborhood offering money and gift cards to those affected. It soon became apparent with the volunteers that giving freely was the rule, not than the exception.

Much to my surprise, the expressions of love and charity had only just begun. There was a throng of people who came to provide assistance, provisions, and support for those of us who found ourselves to be in less fortunate circumstances.

I had anticipated there would be some organized efforts to provide relief and assistance, but I could never have anticipated the vastness of the groups and individuals who were not organized in any way who began filling the streets. They were our neighbors from down the street, across town, or from towns and cities nearby.

And with them, they brought many types of food – hot and cold, pastries, snacks and coolers full of drinks. There were hats, gloves, medical supplies, clothing, baby supplies, pet food, pet supplies, tarps, tools, sunscreen, personal hygiene products, and more supplies than you could find in most small stores.

At one point, there were so many volunteers in the streets that military people were stationed at the intersections, directing traffic. All of these volunteers were a Godsend. It didn't matter what we needed, they either had it or they would go somewhere to get it and bring it back to us.

A piece of steel beam from St. Mary's Church dropped in our house
from the roof structure to the left of the cross - see picture opposite page

A figurine that was pulled from the wreckage
(more color photos, stories & information available at www.jthoh.com)

Chapter 4

The Salvation Army had just opened a new thrift store directly across the street from us a few months earlier. It had previously been a bar and grill, so we were excited when it changed ownership. It was great living across the street because we have always enjoyed shopping at thrift stores. In fact, that's how I came to have so many medical devices, including the CAM boot.

The thrift store had been hit pretty hard, with much of the building demolished and most of what remained was slightly unstable. When the tornado was raining vehicles in our neighborhood, it dropped one inside the building. There, amongst the racks of clothing, sat a crushed silver pickup truck.

Salvation Army thrift store across the street

Immediately after the storm, the Salvation Army rallied its troops and set up a relief center, complete with a couple of circus sized tents, portapotties, and hand washing stations. There were volunteers who came in from all over the country to help serve meals and assist with other immediate needs of the community.

For breakfast, there were usually donuts, snack cakes, fruit, etc., like what you might find at a free breakfast buffet in a motel.

There were always lots of drinks, from bottled water to iced tea to sports drinks. They usually served up something hot and freshly prepared for lunch and dinner. It was a real blessing to be able to walk across the street and have access to such a great relief center.

Salvation Army relief center across the street

Because of the large number of people they were serving, much of the food appeared to be donated. What was served on any given day was prepared from what had been donated a day or two before. This made for some interesting combinations of food that you probably wouldn't find together in a typical meal. Don't get me wrong, the food was very tasty and filling, just sometimes interesting combinations.

Eating regular meals at the relief center was a humbling and awakening experience for me. I had grown up living a pretty comfortable, albeit modest life. Sure, I had my ups and downs just like most people, but there had never been any circumstances in my life that would necessitate seeking help from any relief organization or network. It wasn't that I was too proud, I just simply never had the need.

This is how the less fortunate survive, I thought, finding myself to be now among the ranks of the less fortunate and literally being homeless. I had to pause to take it all in so I could appreciate just how wonderful a hot meal could taste! I was surrounded by many others just as homeless, savoring a spoonful of polish sausage with a spoonful of white rice and a spoonful of green beans, served on a styrofoam plate, with a snack sized bag of yogurt covered raisins for dessert. Clearly, this was another eye opening blessing and life changing moment for me!

Another fortunate aspect of being across the street from the relief center was that it was a gathering point for the various groups and their leaders to meet over meal periods. That meant I could gather information directly from the source, rather than relying upon speculation, conjecture and the constant rumors that ran rampant in the streets.

When the Army Corp of Engineers started working in our neighborhood, I found the person in charge. Believe it or don't, his name was Ronald McDonald. When it came to the cleanup project though, he wasn't *clowning* around and got the crews lined out and working efficiently.

I was somewhat expecting that the guy in charge would be some hard-nosed, bossy kind of a jerk who would be difficult to deal with. Quite to the contrary, Mr. McDonald was very amiable and pleasant to deal with. He gave me his business card with his contact information and told me that if I had any problems or needed anything to let him know.

Surprisingly, I never had to call him, because the crews did such a great job. The volunteers and residents filled the curbs with mounds of debris and just as quickly as they were full, the crews were back hauling it off again. The whole cleanup process functioned quite efficiently and effectively, especially considering the volume of debris that needed to be removed.

Shortly thereafter, another supervisor with the Corp showed up.

He was former military and had served in previous wartime engagements. While we chatted, he carefully surveyed the landscape, calculating how many bombs it would take and how many days of bombing would be required to duplicate the vastness of destruction he was seeing. He figured it would take an astronomical amount of effort and firepower to duplicate it.

"I've been all over the world," he said, "in war and natural disasters, but I've never seen a destructive force like this. I would have expected the death toll to be much greater than what it is."

That comment seemed to be another resounding observation... that through such destruction, relatively few lives were lost. God really had blessed Joplin!

Walking back to the house, I noticed the pilgrims had arrived to dig through some of their rubble. They each made their way slowly and cautiously through the piles of busted up building materials and debris, being careful to avoid all the rusty nails. I walked over to meet them, wanting to see how my granddaughters were doing.

Safely perched in her father's arms, Grace looked up at me and said, "Grandpa, your house is broken!"

"You're right Punkin' Head," I said, rubbing her head and giving her a kiss on the cheek.

"Punkin' Head" was my nickname for her, due to her pumpkin orange hair. "Tater" was the nickname I had for her sister, Olivia, who was a little butterball baby with big round eyes and a face just as round.

Looking around at our *broken* house, it dawned on me just how broken things really were. Not only was our home destroyed, but all the fruit trees, grape vines, berry bushes, strawberry beds, and garden were also completely demolished.

If you've ever used a grass trimmer (e.g. weed whacker, etc.), you'll have a better idea of what I'm talking about. If you're using it on something soft, like grass, the trimmer will cut it cleanly. However, if you use it on something bigger, thicker or tougher, like a tree sapling or big weed, it doesn't cut it cleanly. Instead, it beats it apart and leaves a frayed stump sticking out of the ground.

That's exactly what it looked like, in every direction. Whether it was the trees (big and small), the blackberries, raspberries, grapes, or whatever we had planted, it all looked the same. It was as if a giant grass trimmer had come through and beat the plants to pieces, leaving frayed stumps everywhere.

Of all the trees in the neighborhood, there was one very unique tree in our back yard. It was a maple tree that was originally about twenty-five to thirty feet tall. There were several other maple trees in our neighborhood, about the same size.

Tree with bark stripped in a corkscrew pattern, the trunk twisted off at the top

If you stood by our maple tree and looked to the north, the trees in the next lots over had the bark stripped off the south side of the trees. If you looked at the trees to the south of us, the bark on the north side of the tree was stripped clean. That meant the vortex of the tornado was somewhere between those sets of trees.

The tree in our yard that was right next to the driveway where the Rondo went missing, did not have bark stripped from the north or south side of the tree. Instead, starting at ground level there was a foot-wide strip of bark that was peeled off the tree in a corkscrew pattern all the way up and around the tree. About twelve feet off the ground the wood grain of the trunk and remaining branches had been twisted off, rather than broken.

Abby and Stacey found the license plate and holder, but not the car

The only way that could have happened, was if that tree had been in the middle of the vortex. The debris being sucked off the ground was like a sand blaster, peeling the bark away as it rose from the ground and spun around and upward, inside the vortex.

That's why we couldn't find the Rondo... because it was sucked up in the vortex and carried away. That's why the things in the center of the rooms were missing and the things in the corners of the rooms stayed. Because the things in the corner were outside the circular path of the vortex, they couldn't be sucked up.

The area immediately outside the vortex would have blown everything against the walls and into the corners of the rooms while it sucked up and out what was in the middle of the rooms.

Thinking about it, Grace couldn't have been more accurate in saying that our house was broken. It wasn't just our house that was broken, but our way of life. All that we had worked so hard for was either missing, broken and busted up, imbedded with tornado debris and sludge, or decimated by the rain.

I guess the only thing that wasn't broken was our spirits. People would come by to offer assistance, to pray with us and for us, or just to give encouragement. Most of them were surprised at how positive we were in spite of our very unfortunate circumstances.

Tim found the pilgrims' hard drive - Tiffany and Grace looking on

I was often asked how we could get up every morning and come back to the war zone that was once our home... our castle. How could we go on, knowing that we had lost so much and suffered such a devastating blow?

The answer was really quite simple. When we raced down into the basement and the tornado was directly over the top of us, each of us considered the possibility that we might very well be living our last few moments on earth. Once the tornado had passed and we realized that we had pretty much lost everything but our lives, it was obvious how insignificant our possessions really were in the big scheme of things. We had been liberated from materialism in a matter of minutes.

When asked this question, I would tell people that in reality, we were the lucky ones because our lives and attitudes toward life and family had forever been changed for the better. I could replace the big screen TV above the fireplace mantle, but I could never replace the love I saw in Stacey's eyes when she gazed lovingly into mine.

In the end, losing it all was a very cleansing experience. As the saying goes, "the most important things in life really aren't things" and truer words were never spoken.

"What happened to *your* house," I asked Grace.

"It blew away," she said, shrugging her shoulders, "we don't have a house any more."

"It's okay," I said, rubbing her head, "we're all going to get different houses and we'll plant more strawberries and you can help me pick them again."

She seemed to like that idea... and so did I. You really don't know (and maybe don't appreciate) what you've got, even the simplest of things, until they're taken away from you. Something as simple as picking fruit with my granddaughter had suddenly become priceless and I cherished those memories.

You can almost see the commercial playing out in your mind... *Losing everything you ever had – hundreds of thousands of dollars. Cost to the community – over a billion dollars. Picking and eating fresh fruit with your granddaughter – priceless*!

Focusing back on the work, there wasn't much for the pilgrims to pick through, because their house was completely missing. While some of the structure of our house survived, theirs was completely gone. The only thing that could be found was the hardwood floor that had been sucked off the foundation, slammed against our house, and crumpled in a pile between the two lots.

The pilgrims' floor was sucked off the foundation and slammed into our house

We took a break from our digging to talk to the pilgrims for a few minutes. I was curious what Adam had seen the evening of the storm since he was the last person to come in and rush down into the basement.

"So, Adam, considering the tornado hit us just seconds after you came running inside, what exactly did you see?"

"Well," he said, stretching his arms from left to right, "there was a huge, black wall as far as I could see in either direction, with things flying all around in it."

"Are you kidding me? That was the tornado! Don't you think that would've been some good information to pass along to me as you ran by, headed for the basement?"

"I did tell you."

"All you said was, 'get downstairs' as you ran by, and I thought you were just being a sissy. If you would've told me you saw a tornado, you'd be my hero. You could have been the one who saved my life, but you missed your chance!"

Adam knew I was just kidding. I like to pick at him every chance I get. He knows it's all in fun and he picks back occasionally too.

"I'm okay with that," he said, "you finally figured it out on your own and made it to the basement."

"Just so you know Adam, you're not in my will or life insurance policy, so I'm worth more to you alive... just remember that!"

"Hey dad," Tiffany chimed in, "I lost my wedding set in the tornado. I took it off when I was pulling the pork apart for the tacos. That's when Adam saw the tornado warnings on the TV. He grabbed the girls, pushed me out the door, and I didn't think to grab it. We're going to look for it but if anyone comes over to help, tell them to keep an eye out for it."

"Not a problem," I said, "but considering that your whole house is missing, I wouldn't hold out much hope of finding anything."

"I know, but we're going to look anyway."

Just then, a pickup truck stopped in the street.

88

"We've got MRE's (Meals Ready to Eat), cheeseburgers, chips and drinks," yelled a man sitting in the back who was surrounded by coolers and cardboard boxes filled with assorted bags of chips. We took him up on the offer and he tossed us a bag of miniature candy bars for dessert.

With the exception of the back steps that had been swept clean, we preferred to stand while we ate. There weren't many areas to sit without risking injury or getting sludge all over yourself. My feet were already full of nail holes and the last thing I wanted was a rusty nail in my rear end or the sludge ruining any of the few items of clothing I had!

Lunch break - Me, Stacey, Heather, Abby and Grace

When we were finishing up with our lunch, I noticed the kids dropping their wrappers and empty drink bottles on the ground.

"What are you doing?" I grunted, pointing to the trash they had just dropped on the ground.

"What?" Abby asked, looking around, seemingly oblivious to the intent of my question.

"You dropped your trash on the ground, so pick it up and throw it in a trash bag."

"Dad, we just went through a tornado, look around, there's trash everywhere!"

"That's tornado trash... we had no control over how it came to be, so it gets to lay where it is. The human trash we have control over, so pick it up and put it in a trash bag. We may be rednecks but we're not hillbillies, and there *is* a difference!"

When everybody went back to work digging through the rubble, I rounded up some fifty-five gallon barrels and used them as trash cans around the property.

Abby and Ashley looking for anything salvageable

Later in the day, the pilgrims left and returned shortly thereafter with some large plastic bags full of used clothes that had been donated. I piled them into the trunk of the rental car to sort through once we got back to Arkansas.

Because Stacey and I routinely shopped at thrift stores, we were accustomed to wearing used clothes and having used items around the house. The girls, on the other hand, were experiencing something new. We all found clothes in the bag that fit us and we were very thankful to have them.

When we returned home at the end of the day, my mother-in-law, Dianne handed us some bags that contained new clothes for each of us. There were t-shirts and pants for everyone and dress clothes for me, including shirts, shoes, ties, and a belt. There were also boxes of hair dryers and straightening irons for Stacey and the girls. It had all been donated by Jim, the family friend who had come with Tim to rescue us the night of the tornado.

The next day I proudly wore my newly donated and slightly used clothes during the daily cleanup. About mid morning, I walked across the street to the Salvation Army to get Stacey and me a cold drink. The line was about a dozen people, which wasn't bad. There were many times the end of the line extended well beyond the big tent, way out into the parking lot.

I'm one of those people who's somewhat reserved around others I don't know and often keep to myself, so being at the back of the line suits me just fine. As I was approaching the first table that had an assortment of chips and other snacks, one of the volunteers at the table, a man in his fifties, walked directly up to me, into my personal space. With a big grin on his face, he yelled, "Roll Tide!"

What the heck, I thought, *is he talking to me?*

I looked around to see if anyone had walked up behind me and maybe he was talking to them. Nope... he was talking to me!

"Roll Tide!" he yelled again.

"Are you talking to me?" I asked hesitantly.

"Yeah," he said, and still smiling, poked me in my somewhat rounded and protruding belly.

I looked down and saw that I was wearing an *Alabama Crimson Tide* t-shirt. I was not familiar with any Alabama collegiate sports etiquette, so I was still confused. I explained to him that the shirt had been donated to me.

"What am I supposed to say or do when someone yells, 'Roll Tide' to me?"

He smiled even bigger.

"You yell, 'Roll Tide' back to them!"

"That's it?"

"Yep."

"Okay then... Roll Tide!" I yelled confidently, with a big, cheesy grin on my face.

"You've got it now," he said, shaking my hand and patting me heartily on the back.

Proceeding through the line to the drink station, all I could think was, *what a great country, and how about those folks from Alabama... they're great people!*

My Alabama t-shirt had become my new favorite, even though I'd never spent any time there. Every time I wore it, I felt a connection with the people from Tuscaloosa who had lost lives and had their properties twisted and splintered by a tornado only a month before. To me, it was a tribute to their suffering and hope, honoring the triumph of their spirit just as much as ours.

As we continued digging through our rubble we were met with even more volunteers. It was like they were coming out of the woodwork! Not only were we being catered to as far as food, drinks, and supplies, but people were showing up with gloves on their hands, offering to help us dig through our debris.

Tim watches as people begin to fill the streets, offering help to others

Because we were mostly interested in our own personal effects and memorabilia, we turned away a lot of volunteers who wanted to help us the first few days. It's not that we didn't appreciate the offer, we simply felt it would be better for us to find and salvage what was meaningful to us and what wasn't.

Wave after wave of people came, offering help, praying with us, trying to cheer us up, and generally providing any type of support we needed. They were everywhere in the neighborhood, helping anyone who would let them be of any assistance.

I was so moved by this outpouring of compassion that I went downstairs and grabbed my can of black spray paint. I knew that I couldn't personally thank everyone who came by, but I wanted to let them know how grateful we were for their many selfless acts of service and love.

I climbed on the pile of crumpled hardwood flooring that had blown in from the pilgrims' house. On the south side of our house, the brick had been stripped clean and exposed the twelve inch solid wood boards underneath. It was there that I wrote, "Thank You Volunteers We ♥ U!"

I tend to be an optimistic person and I try to see the good in things and find a positive spin. However, I think I had become a little bit jaded in respect to humanity in general. There's a country western song that says you find out who your *real* friends are when the chips are down. I had generally subscribed to the notion that unless they are your really good friends, you may not be able to count on very many people when the chips are down.

My fourth message spray painted on the south wall

However, I could not have been more wrong about my fellow neighbors, countrymen and women. I was totally flabbergasted by the numbers of people who just kept coming and coming and coming. I met more good people in those first few days than most people will ever meet in a lifetime.

Over the course of a few short days, my general view of humanity had taken a one hundred eighty degree turn around. On a daily basis, I would think of the words of another country western song where the singer says he saw God today in the actions of others. Clearly, I saw God every day, all day, and lots of his angels throughout the day!

To say that I was in awe of the volunteers would be an understatement. I've never been so moved with so many positive emotions in all my life. Throughout the day I thought about the message I had spray painted on the wall and reasoned that "love" was not a big enough word or symbol to express what I was feeling from and for all those wonderful people.

I went back to the basement to get my can of spray paint. I ran back to the south wall and beneath my previous message, I wrote, "YOU ARE OUR HEROES!"

Without a doubt, the volunteers were, are, and forever will be our heroes. I could never find the words to completely convey the great love, admiration, appreciation, gratitude, and respect I have for all the wonderful people who blessed our family and the entire community in our darkest hour!

I don't like to ask for (or accept) help, unless it's unavoidable or something I can't do myself. However, the enormity of the task was so overwhelming I knew that I could never get things done without lots and lots of help. We had salvaged about as many personal items as we could, so we stopped turning away the volunteers who were so eager to provide assistance.

One of the first organized groups of volunteers who came was the Helping Hands. There were about a dozen of them, men and teenagers. They had a schedule of locations they would be working that day.

"We're here to help in whatever way you need us," said Russ, one of the adult leaders, "you're first on the list. Just tell us what you need and we'll get started on it."

One of the Helping Hands groups that came to our aid

We had a lot of items stored down in our basement... literally tons of stuff. That's probably a lot of the reason why our flimsy garage door didn't blow completely in, because there was so much stuff packed in front of it.

We had a crawl space about three and a half feet above the basement floor, with about that much clearance inside. From front to back were lots of heavy items inside large plastic storage tubs.

Not only was there a limited amount of room to crawl around up there, but I had originally put down several layers of plastic, covered with several layers of carpet before ever storing anything there. I did that so it wouldn't be so rough on my hands and knees when I had to go up there and crawl around.

Because it had rained about a foot the previous couple of days, there was standing water on top of the soaked carpet. Needless to say, the crawl space was pretty nasty and full of sludge soup.

"If there is any way possible you could get the stuff from the crawl space out," I said, "we could load it in the storage unit."

No sooner were the words out of my mouth than a handful of men climbed up and started slogging through the crawl space, dragging the tubs down to the others waiting below.

The group formed a line from the basement out to the back driveway, making quick work of clearing out the heavy items. I was much relieved to have that done and out of the way, knowing that my bad back would prevent me from doing it myself.

"What's next?" Russ asked.

"That's pretty good for right now," I said, relieved to have that much done.

"We're here now," he insisted, "so tell me what you want us to do next."

I could see where this was headed. He knew there was more that could be done to help and he was determined to accomplish as much as possible before they had to leave. Some of the things that remained in the basement were lighter items that needed to be boxed up, which our kids could do later.

"If you don't mind and have the time, the rest of these heavy things need to go," I said, pointing to the other things that needed to come out and either loaded into storage or hauled off to the alley.

"Not a problem," he said, organizing the group into action.

It wasn't long before they had the majority of the basement cleared out. It was easy to see who had been up in the crawl space as their clothes were soaked with dark brown, chunky tornado sludge soup.

I doubted that even the best laundry detergent, presoak, and oxygenated cleaners were going to make a dent in cleaning them. Those clothes probably needed to go into a toxic waste disposal.

"Are you sure there's nothing else we can do for you?"

I assured Russ that they had done as much as could be done at that point.

"Let me know if you need us to come back, and don't be shy in asking!"

He and the rest of the group thanked me for allowing them to serve us. Their warm and genuine smiles reassured me that the offer for additional help was more than just lip service. I knew that if I asked, they would be back at a moment's notice, willing and able.

Found in the rubble - "Finding Forever Love," by T. A. Llynn
(more color photos, stories & information available at www.jthoh.com)

Chapter 5

In the early days of relief effort, not much had been cleared from the neighborhoods. Our yard and every yard around us was covered in layers of building materials, housing wire, downed power lines, sheet metal, whole vehicles and parts of vehicles, bricks, trees, broken glass, gardening tools, hand tools, TVs, sinks, water heaters, and an assortment of other miscellaneous stuff that was now trash or debris.

There was all kinds of nasty stuff floating around in the air that probably wasn't healthy to breathe in and any time the wind blew, even more of it whipped up into the air. Any time someone wanted to take a break, they had to sit amid all this noxious rubble.

It was at this time, I decided that I wanted to make a place where the volunteers could sit and take a break away from the noxious rubble, instead of on top of it. The couch in our living room had been trapped under a wall that had fallen on it. After the wall was removed, I was able to get it out and move it to the curb near the front of the house.

I recovered the love seat as well, but I was missing cushions and pillows from the couch and love seat. Over the course of a couple of days, I would wander around the neighborhood and look in the debris piles that the neighbors were clearing from their yards and piling by the street. During this time, I was able to retrieve all the cushions and two of the four pillows that had originally been with the furniture.

I didn't have any place to set the furniture inside the structure of the house because it was still so full of debris. I left the couch and love seat next to the street so that at least there would be a comfortable place for some volunteers or people passing by to sit.

After the deluge of rain we had initially, it turned to sunny, hot, and humid. Once the furniture had dried, it was encrusted with thick, baked on tornado sludge. I grabbed one of the many sticks that were everywhere, and began beating on the cushions and pillows, trying to de-sludge everything so it wouldn't be so nasty to sit on.

The love seat after I had beaten the sludge out of it, sitting next to the street

While I was beating the furniture, a supervisor from the Army Corp of Engineers came over and struck up a conversation. He then advised me of a company he was confident could come and steam clean my furniture, making it as good as new.

Even though my only purpose for the furniture was going to be sitting out in the elements for the volunteers, I was tickled by his thoughtfulness. He apparently believed that I was going to try to salvage the beat-up, sludged-up furniture and wanted to offer some furniture restoration insights.

"Do you think they could get all this baked on sludge out of it," I asked, breaking off some bigger chunks of hardened sludge.

"Oh yeah," he said, "they've got really nice steam cleaning equipment. They'll get you fixed right up and good as new in no time... and they're affordable."

I thanked him for his insight and wondered to myself what it must be like for him and the others who had come into such devastation. How many others like him tried to help out in their own ways, while still engaged in the job they were sent to do? Considering that he wasn't there to help me clean my furniture and had to stay on top of the crews he supervised, it made me feel good to know that he saw an opportunity to help someone in need and took it.

Shortly thereafter, a convoy of passenger vans full of mostly teenagers and a few adult leaders pulled up and stopped in the street. A couple of the adults jumped out and asked if they could help. I welcomed their help and thanked them for stopping by.

One of the leaders, Richard, asked if he could offer up a prayer.

"Certainly," I said, "that would be wonderful."

The leaders and youth gathered all around me and Richard offered up a very touching prayer for me, my family, and the community.

"Father," he said in conclusion, "please heal Tim, his family, and the community, physically, emotionally and spiritually, and provide for their many needs, we pray in Jesus' name, amen."

They wasted no time and went straight to work, clearing debris and moving it to the curb, not only in our lot but the pilgrims' lot and the lot next to theirs.

One of the biggest accomplishments of the day was clearing the debris from the bedroom with the neon green wall that had "GOD BLESS JOPLIN!" written on it. This meant I finally had a place to put some furniture and make a real resting place for the volunteers.

I swept off most of the remaining broken glass, small debris, and dirt from the hardwood floors as best I could. I then solicited the help of a couple of the volunteers to move the big pieces of furniture onto the cleaned floor.

Getting furniture set up – couch (center) and table leaning on its side (right)

Our coffee table originally had a glass top, which was broken, so I put a broken piece of kitchen countertop over it. I completed the ensemble with two wooden TV trays, used as end tables.

This group worked tirelessly for the remainder of the day until the sun was heading down over the horizon. When they started circling around the vans that brought them, I hurried over to their group, wanting to thank everyone for helping us.

Before I could get the words out of my mouth, each and every one of them came up and shook my hand or hugged me. They thanked me... for the *blessing* of letting them come and spend the day doing hard labor in the hot sun.

"Thank you so much," I said, as they climbed into their vans, "God bless you!" Watching them drive away, all I could see was smiling, dust covered faces peering through the windows.

Once there was a safe path from the sidewalk to the *green room*, more people began signing the wall and leaving messages. At first it was a signature here and there, but before long, signatures and messages were popping up everywhere on the wall.

The next day, on the outskirts of Joplin, Tawny reached for her alarm clock and silenced it. She was anxious to begin her day that would start with assembling care packages. They were for the people whose homes and lives had been devastated. After a quick shower, she slipped into a pair of jeans, a t-shirt, and sneakers, and headed to the spare bedroom.

Along the way, she passed multiple stacks of boxes that had been sent to her home from various parts of the country. It meant a lot to her that many of the boxes had come from her hometown of Lovell, Wyoming. When friends and family had heard of the destruction, they didn't waste any time and just started sending things they knew people would need.

There had been days when the package delivery person would pile so many boxes on the front porch, that it was impassable. The donations had already filled two rooms of her house and were coming in faster than she could get them delivered.

Placing items from the various boxes into individual bags, she reflected upon the tragedy and how it affected her neighbors, the community. The loss and suffering of so many had given her a keener perspective of life.

Possessions and material things are meaningless in comparison to those you love, she thought, *and there really is no place like home. Your children's friends who were at your house the day before, could be gone forever. A cross word spoken to another can hurt you deeply if you never get a chance to take it back. A teenager you didn't think much of previously, can become a hero in an instant. A city block can mean the difference between life and death. The person you stood behind in the grocery store without acknowledging, may be the one willing to sacrifice their own life for your safety or someone you love.*

Before long, Tawny was joined by one of her adult daughters, Laura who would help assemble and distribute the care packages. As she worked side by side with her mother, her heart ached for the people who were now suffering. It was a feeling with which she was all too familiar.

Care packages were a welcomed gift after having so much lost or ruined

Several years before, Laura had left for college and the beginning of a life of her own. There she fell in love with and married Brett.

She loved it when he would tell her, "you melt like butta' in my hands," and he had always been right about that.

Brett was diagnosed with testicular cancer and for a short time, the radiation, surgery, chemotherapy, and other procedures kept the cancer at bay. But over time, the cancer returned with a vengeance, mercilessly ravaging his body.

Laura was with Brett during his final minutes, holding his hand, trying to comfort him. He held her hand firmly but his grip slowly loosened and eventually, he let go.

Oh, how she missed him, long before those final moments. She was totally and completely in love with him and he loved her back the same. The memories of those times and the strength of that love is what kept her going, and over time, helped her heal.

A tear rolled down her cheek because she knew so intimately, just how much so many people were hurting at that very moment. Her heart ached and went out to those who had lost loved ones, knowing that the road to recovery would be long, and there would be lots of pain and anguish along the way.

"Are you okay?" her mother asked, noticing Laura wiping a tear from her face.

"I just feel so bad for all these people," she said, the tears now flowing freely. "I know how it feels to lose someone you love and it hurts so bad. I wish there was more I could do!"

With tears welling up in her eyes, Tawny dropped the bag from her hand and embraced her daughter tightly, reassuring her that things would eventually get better, and in time, all would heal.

After a good cry, mother and daughter returned to their labor of love, anticipating the joy of delivering their care packages. They looked forward to positively affecting the lives of those with such a great need who were so emotionally and spiritually injured.

As the sun was rising over the war-torn landscape, Tim, Aly, and my niece, Ashley, returned with a group of Helping Hands from the Bentonville / Rogers area. They began clearing the lot of the bigger chunks, such as pieces of walls and roofs that had blown in from other houses.

Tim working with a crew of Helping Hands

There were people everywhere, much like watching ants on an anthill. The work was going smoothly and then there was a scream from the front of the house. I looked over to the living room area where a group of people were beginning to gather around a man with his butt on the floor and only one leg above it. He seemed to be in pain, trying unsuccessfully to pull himself up.

I rushed over to Stacey and told her that one of her brother's crew had apparently broken through the floor where the air vent came up from the basement. I told her to come quickly because I was afraid he might be hurt.

Walking toward the man who was still struggling to get up, I could see that it was her brother, Tim, not one of his crew. With a little effort, we finally got him out of the floor and back on his feet. Stacey examined his leg and foot. Nothing appeared to be broken and there were no cuts, just lots of scrapes, bruising, and swelling.

I quickly moved a slab of concrete that had broken free from the front porch and placed it over the hole in the floor, to prevent a repeat injury.

I couldn't believe it, the only two injuries sustained thus far, were after the tornado and both of the injured were siblings.

"Hey Aly," I said, trying to hold back my laughter, "try to stay clear of Tim and Stacey... it appears that they're accident prone and you might get hurt just being near them!"

"I know," she said, chuckling, "I can't believe they're both hurt and limping around. Should we make them sit in one of the parked cars so they don't get hurt any worse?"

"Okay Tim," I yelled, "you're on light duty with Stacey... stay out of the demolition zone!"

Within minutes, his scraped up leg was turning black and blue, and before long, his knee and ankle had swollen to about twice their normal size. It hurt just looking at his leg.

"You're not going to sue me are you?"

"You're lucky the house is already destroyed," he joked, while grimacing at the same time, "otherwise it would be mine!"

He took a much needed break and went to the store to pick up an adjustable knee brace to secure his ailing leg. He returned about an hour later, propped his leg up on a five gallon bucket and gently placed an ice bag on his knee.

Later on that day, after all the excitement of Tim's injury had subsided, I received a call from Adam.

"Heidi-ho neighbor, I think I found your car."

"Are you kidding, where?"

"About three blocks east, down twenty-fifth street. At least I think it's yours. It looks more like a compact car right now, but it's definitely the right color."

"Sit tight, we'll be right there!"

Adam and Stacey try to determine if this vehicle is the Rondo

I told Stacey about the car and we jumped into the rental car. We drove down the street until we found Adam. He was standing next to a crumpled ball of silver metal and tires, laying in someone's front yard. It looked like it had gone through a car crusher.

We walked around the wreckage a couple of times, trying to ascertain whether it was ours, or just another silver car that had been mangled in the twister. I looked for anything inside that might provide evidence, but there was nothing. Even the glove compartment had been ripped open and its contents emptied out, now gone with the wind.

Finally, we noticed a small decal on the back door of the vehicle that we recognized as being ours. It was the Rondo after all, but it sure didn't look like it.

It had been sucked up in the vortex of the tornado, carried three blocks and dropped in someone's front yard, just like the vehicles that had rained down in our neighborhood. Somewhere along the journey, it was beaten to pieces and crushed.

"At least we can tell the insurance adjuster where to find it," Stacey said, "and get that settled."

We took several pictures and then headed back to the house, where we continued working with the volunteers.

The Rondo that once sat seven passengers is now a compact

At the end of the day, it was time for the Helping Hands to make their way back to the tent city they had erected in an empty field near St. John's hospital. They would sleep there at night and work in various locations throughout the day. I thanked them for all their hard work and again, each of them thanked me for allowing them to serve us.

After several hours of inactivity, Tim's leg was beginning to hit its peak with stiffness, swelling, and pain. He started hobbling ever so slowly toward his pickup truck, ready to return home when Aly offered to drive. He quickly dismissed the notion, assuring her every painful step of the way that he was good to go.

When he was unable to swing his leg up into the driver's side of the truck, he reluctantly handed her the keys. She snickered, watching him limp around the truck to the passenger side where he crawled onto the seat, wincing every inch of the way.

"I'm okay to drive," he protested, gently returning the bag of ice to his knee, "but Aly really wants to drive and I just don't have the energy, after all the hard work today, to argue with her."

"Yeah, we understand," Stacey said, leaning to one side, trying to keep the weight off her injured foot, "I'll probably let Tim drive home too... I don't feel like arguing either!"

Aly and I just laughed and humored both of them in their stricken condition.

Meanwhile, nearly five hundred fifty miles to the south, in Bryan Texas, Evelyn and her family were making plans for vacation. She had graduated High School and attended the after-graduation party. There was lots of bottled water, chips and paper goods left over.

Her mother, Bonita, was on the after-graduation party committee and suggested that their family turn their vacation into a family service project to help out in Joplin. The rest of the family agreed and the committee offered the water, chips, and paper goods to be distributed to those in need.

The next morning the family packed all their clothes, camping gear, and the other supplies into their car. Evelyn couldn't figure out how they were able to make so much stuff fit. Before it was packed in, it seemed as though much of it would have to be left behind. But surprisingly, somehow it all fit. The family piled into the bulging car and pointed it north towards Interstate Forty-Five.

That morning, shortly after we arrived at the house, I looked up from my work to see two women walking toward us. I greeted Tawny and Laura as they walked up the steps into the kitchen.

They told to us how they wanted to help the community and provide a care package for those in need. They gave a bag to Stacey, Tiffany, Abby, and Heather stuffed with lotions and other personal care items. Abby's bag also contained some baby clothes and other baby items she would need in a few short months.

As we visited, Laura seemed especially interested in our experience during and after the storm. We spent some time answering questions, showing her around the house and basement, pointing out the location where we had taken shelter.

It was obvious that she was genuinely committed to providing relief, help, and support in any way she could. Before they departed to make more deliveries, she made us promise that if there was anything at all that we needed, to be sure to call her and let her know.

Watching them drive away, I noticed a large group from the Samaritan's Purse who were working their way through the neighborhood. They had just started on the lot across the street with a crew and a Bobcat loader on tracks.

The previous volunteers had moved a lot of big items and building materials away from our house, but it was difficult to make much headway because there was still so much stuff laying everywhere. I asked the crew if they could use the Bobcat to push some of the debris into a pile, making a clear path to the alley.

Volunteers gather near a Bobcat loader assisting in the cleanup efforts

Within minutes, they were plowing the wreckage into a pile and clearing a path to the alley. The pilgrims were still looking for Tiffany's wedding set but making slow progress because their hardwood floor was still sitting on the piles of debris, preventing them from being searched.

I asked the operator of the Bobcat if he could move the floor and put it on the pile he had just made at the alley. The bucket of the Bobcat had a moving jaw that he could use to clamp down on anything in the bucket.

"No problem," he said, roaring into the hardwood floor with the jaws of his machine wide open.

He was able to grab big chunks of the floor and move them out of the way, which would have taken forever by hand. He offered to move the piles of smaller debris that laid between the pilgrims' foundation and our house, the entire length of the house. We refused his offer, since there was still a freckle of a chance of finding the ring, even though it seemed like an impossible chance.

Debris pile after the bobcat had removed the hardwood floor

The pilgrims and some volunteers began to dig through the debris that had been uncovered by the bobcat. After several hours of digging, the only thing they had to show for their efforts was more dirt and grime.

"Did you find anything," I hollered.

"Not yet," Tiffany said, shaking her head, "we'll keep looking... all I can do is hope."

Later that day as we continued digging through our rubble, I heard a bunch of shouting and celebrating. I stopped what I was doing and ran around to the back of the house. There I found the pilgrims jumping up and down, hugging each other.

Tiffany raised her hand, and low and behold, there was a ring on her finger. *What are the chances*, I thought, while simultaneously holding out more hope that I could find my USB drive that had all my important files on it, including Stacey's book.

"You found it?"

"Just the wedding band," Tiffany said, "but if it's here, maybe we'll find the engagement ring too."

Stacey and I with the furniture set up in what was once Heather's bedroom

Later that day, Tim found the hard drive on which the pilgrims had all their family pictures stored. Even if all the paper pictures were lost, they had everything captured on the hard drive. They seemed happier to have found the hard drive than the wedding ring.

By this time, I was convinced that I was going to find my USB drive. *It's much bigger than a ring and surely I'm entitled to a little bit of good fortune,* I reasoned, *just like the pilgrims.* I went back to inching my way through the debris in our bedroom on my hands and knees, one handful of sludge and crud at a time.

Apparently the pilgrims had as much good luck as they could stand for one day, because they left to run some errands. As for me and my household, we continued to keep on digging, with a little help from our family and our newest friends, the volunteers.

By this time, the cell phone towers were back online for the most part and we could use our phones for both text and talk, incoming and outgoing.

While I was still searching for that elusive USB drive, I got a call from Tiffany.

"Hey dad, I just found out there's a couple of nationally organized volunteer groups that will be coming to town with crews. If you want I can get you on the list for some help."

"How long will they be in town?"

"Through the summer and some even through the winter if necessary."

"Yeah, put me on the list."

I could hear her talking to someone in the background.

"The soonest they can get a crew over to help you is next week, is that okay?"

"Absolutely. You know, beggars can't be choosers and I'll take any help I can get at this point."

"Okay, you're on the list. I'll bring some release forms for you to sign before they can start on the property."

"Cool, you know where to find me."

The talk on the street was that the city had a deadline for property cleanup. If your lot wasn't cleaned of the debris and clutter surrounding (but not necessarily inside) the structure, you were in jeopardy of being fined for every day you were out of compliance. There was no doubt that our property was clearly not up to standards and the deadline was looming out there.

Thank God for the volunteers, I thought, *I'm glad to be on the list for their help. It's unfortunate that they won't be here for a few more days, but I'm sure there will be others who will come by to offer assistance.*

I needed a break and a cold drink, so I walked across the street with Stacey to use the portapotties and get something to wet my whistle.

By now, the relief center had grown to include free chiropractic adjustments, massage therapy, acupuncture, and a tetanus shot station. It was great to see so many people offering to help and provide relief in any way possible.

"Would you like to have some acupuncture therapy," one of the therapists asked.

"No thanks," I said, "I'm trying to recover from the *accidental* acupuncture in my feet from all the rusty nails. I think I've got enough holes in my body for right now. But, I do think it works, because after all these holes in my feet, I can actually hear better."

116

I couldn't really hear better, I was just teasing the acupuncture therapists. It's not that I wasn't appreciative of their offer, it's just that I don't like needles and I would have a hard time with having more pins and needles stuck all over my body.

The green wall filling with messages - Photo used with permission:

Later in the day, a newspaper reporter and photographer came by and wanted to visit with us. They wanted to see inside the house and in the basement where we rode out the tornado. We took them through the house and recounted the minutes leading up to the tornado and immediately afterwards.

Stacey told them that during the tornado, she felt herself being levitated off the floor and being pulled toward the stairwell when the tornado was directly on top of us. She was standing close to the stairwell and told how she had to grab ahold of some steel plumbing pipes to keep herself in place.

The last part of the "house tour" was showing them where the door at the top of the stairs had been closed off with the 2x4 board and piece of rebar.

"The ceiling here," I said, pointing to the pieces of lath that were still attached above the stairwell, "is the only part remaining in the whole house. We were all trapped inside, with no way out and the gas was leaking."

It then occurred to me, as if a light bulb had just been turned on... we weren't really trapped inside. Instead, we had been kept safe inside of what was nothing less than a protective cocoon.

Even though I had not taken the time to close the door behind me when I raced down the stairs, it somehow closed. Then, the 2x4 board and the piece of rebar that shot through the walls kept it from opening.

The ceiling stayed intact, unlike the rest of the ceiling in the house. All of these things together kept the debris from pounding down on top of us during the crushing phases of the tornado (both coming and going), and kept us from being sucked out when the vortex came over the top of us.

What are the odds of that happening exactly that way, I wondered, *just by chance?* From that point on, my story went from *being trapped downstairs*, to *thinking we were trapped downstairs, but really being sheltered in a protective cocoon of God's love*.

And speaking of God's love, I can't tell you how many people, whether with a group or just individuals walking through the neighborhood, wanted to just stop and pray for us. People walking and driving by, who were praying for us, was not only amazing, but spiritually, emotionally, and mentally uplifting. It was both rejuvenating and strengthening to the soul.

How many times, I wondered, *do you have millions and millions of people thinking about you, praying for you, and wishing well for you, individually and as a community, like we did?*

That evening, the sun was just setting over the horizon of what had been a very long, hot, humid, and dirty day's work for all of us. The volunteers had gone for the day, Stacey was covering things in the basement with a large tarp and I was walking through the house looking for any tools that needed to be put away.

Messages on bedroom wall

A car slowly came to a stop in the street in front of the house. This happened all the time, so I didn't pay much attention. I think that most people took me for a volunteer who was there cleaning up. Continuing through the house, I noticed a woman who was walking directly towards me.

119

She appeared to be in her middle forties, nicely dressed in dark slacks and a light pastel blue blouse, with her shoulder length hair neatly fixed. The heels of her shoes clicked and clacked as she strode across the hardwood floors.

"Is this your house," she asked as she approached me.

"What's left of it," I said, looking around at what was becoming a shell of mostly 2x4 stud framework.

"I'm Karen," she said extending her hand.

"I'm Tim," I said, grabbing her hand and shaking it, "it's nice to meet you."

"I had hoped I would find you here."

"Really?"

Tears began to well up in her eyes as she continued. "I had lost hope. I lost everything in the tornado and I was finding it difficult to go on. I drove by your house one evening, saw the writing on the walls and stopped. I started to read the messages and I could feel the presence of God and angels in your house. Now I come here every couple of nights, just to feel God's love and enjoy the presence of His angels inside your house."

She began brushing back the tears that were streaming down her cheeks.

"Your house gives me hope. I've been praying, hoping to catch you here, and thank you."

"You don't need to thank me," I said, feeling a lump welling up in my throat, "I'm just happy to know that it could make such a positive difference for you."

120

"You have no idea!"

During our visit, she wanted to make sure that it was okay for her to come back and wander through the house on a regular basis. I assured her that it was absolutely fine, and to come by any time she felt the need.

The first angel at the house we could actually see with our eyes

Meeting Karen was a very gratifying experience that I will never forget. The simple act of leaving messages on the walls of this house by myself and many of the volunteers, somehow provided the spiritual catalyst for her to begin the healing process.

It wasn't anything grand or complicated. There was no fanfare... no spectacle... simply the heartfelt messages of faith, hope, and love, left by others that would be just the right medicine for an injured and ailing soul.

Driving back to Arkansas that evening, a warm, comfortable feeling began filling my heart and I experienced a profound sense of peace as I pondered upon Karen's story.

I was amazed at how something so simple could have such a profound effect on a person's whole outlook on life. At this point, I knew of at least two people who were beginning to heal... Karen and myself.

It soon became very apparent that the two of us weren't the only ones affected by the messages that covered the walls. Because I worked at the house frequently, many more people came by to tell me of similar feelings and experiences.

Angels that appeared on some of the wall studs

I was told repeatedly by strangers off the street, how they had experienced a spiritual manifestation, many of them receiving some sort of spiritual healing while inside the walls of the house. Over and over, testimonies were freely born by people who felt the undeniable presence of God and His angels protecting the house and blessing the community.

"I know that God sent angels to protect you and your family,"

122

another woman told me, "and I know they're still here, protecting this house from vandalism. I know this house was full of love before the tornado and I can feel that it's full of love now. I pray for it every day, and I know God will keep his angels watching over it until every heart in Joplin has healed."

A butterfly drawn on a wall stud

There had been a spiritual manifestation and awakening during the storm. Many people in the community, especially children, reported seeing butterflies and butterfly people throughout the storm and afterwards. Most often, the stories were about how the butterfly people had saved and protected them and their family members from harm and danger. In some of the stories, the butterfly people were taking men and women up into the sky.

If it had been an isolated incident, any skeptic could almost write it off as the vivid imagination of a child. However, when you consider the numerous reports and the consistencies between the stories of the children and the stories I heard firsthand from many adults, it would be extremely difficult to discount or discredit what they experienced and the protection and healing they received.

A butterfly painted on a wall stud

Not only did I hear of the butterfly people and angels in and around our house, but they began symbolically appearing. First, there was a cardboard angel that was hung in the hall closet. There were several angels and a butterfly drawn on a few of the wall studs. Later, there were many more painted throughout the house.

I'm led to believe that these symbols were left by people who knew there really were angels watching over Joplin and our house.

Not only was there no vandalism to speak of, but just the opposite was true. There were several "improvements" that were made over the course of time by unknown contributors, including flowers, decorations, pictures, etc.

One day I found a rosary that someone had carefully hung on a nail near a hole in the wall on the south side. Occasionally, the furniture was neatly rearranged in the living room area.

A dream was left in the china hutch and a reminder that "Divided we fall, Together we stand. One town fell, But a nation will rebuild it!!!"

On another occasion, someone brought a busted up plaque that originally said, "Dream" with the "m" missing at the end. They placed it in the china cabinet, against the wall and completed it by drawing the "m" on the wall with a marker.

Shortly after memorial day someone placed an American flag in the bricks stacked out in front of the house. After it had become very tattered from the weather, it was changed out with a new flag later in the fall.

Many volunteers came to personally thank me, because our house gave them a place and an opportunity to leave a message of hope that others could read after they left town.

Originally, they would ask permission to write on the walls, but over time, they knew that no permission was required.

There were many times when I would be working around the house, in the yard, or in the basement and hear the voices of a group of volunteers who had come to be inspired or inspire others.

At times, there was a constant flow of pedestrians and motorists alike who came by to take pictures of the house and the messages on the walls. There were many times I was asked to take pictures for people who wanted to be photographed in front of the house.

Angel painted on the living room wall
(more color photos, stories & information available at www.jthoh.com)

Chapter 6

Across town, Evelyn and her family were just arriving as the sun peaked at the hottest part of the day. They dropped off their supplies and asked where they might be able to provide assistance. They were given our address as a good place to start.

Stacey, the girls, and I had retreated downstairs to escape the blistering hot sun that showed no signs of letting up. We had gathered some cardboard boxes from local businesses that morning and were taping them together so we could pack some of the things we wanted to save.

We heard some chatter from the side of the house as a group of people made their way around to the back. Coming around the corner were two parents and three teenagers, all wearing bright yellow Helping Hands t-shirts.

"Are you the Bartows?" the father asked.

"Yes we are," I said, stepping forward to shake his hand. "This is my wife Stacey, our daughters Abby and Heather, and Abby's friend, Taylor."

"Pleased to meet you," he said, with a hint of southern drawl, "I'm Doug, this is my wife Bonita, the kids are Evelyn, Christopher, and Chester. We contacted the church and were told that you might need some help, so we're here to do whatever we can for you."

"We were about to go on vacation," Bonita interjected, "but when we heard what happened here, we knew this is where the Lord wanted us to be."

"Where ya from?" I asked.

"Bryan, Texas" was the reply.

"Are you sure you want to spend your family vacation digging through that stuff out there in the scorching sun? I can promise you it's really nasty work!"

"We're used to hard work," Doug assured me, "and being from Texas, this heat don't bother us!"

"If you're sure that's what you want to do, and if your kids don't mind, we'd love to have you."

Messages on bedroom closet wall

Evelyn was beginning to feel the excitement of being able to help. Back when hurricane Katrina and Rita had hit the gulf coast, she was too young to volunteer. This would be her first opportunity to help in a serious disaster area.

Here she was, miles from home, helping people she had never met and knew nothing about them, except that they were in real need of assistance that she could provide. She was motivated not only by the destruction she saw everywhere and heartfelt sympathy for others, but the constant thought of being in the shoes of those who had all their worldly possessions literally ripped apart.

When she and her family began the arduous task of digging through piles of rubble, she felt invigorated by the challenge to find something here and there that was worth saving. In a way, it was like a treasure hunt. Even though the treasures weren't hers, they still needed to be found.

With each new find she felt more energized to find additional treasures. The heat and dust that permeated the air sucked the strength out of her. Still, she hated taking breaks knowing that other valuables remained, waiting to be discovered.

Continuing on with the treasure hunt, she unearthed many new baby clothes that were still in great condition, they just needed some cleaning. She uncovered many other personal items and belongings.

Many times during her work, she had to carry boards and bricks off to the curb so she could continue searching for lost artifacts.

Every day she and her family returned, it was more of the same. Even though it was a hot, dirty, and messy job, she had no complaints. She was there to get the job done and knew the project wasn't about her, but rather those she had come to serve. Keeping that thought foremost in her mind made the boards, bricks, and buckets of debris lighter and easier to carry.

At the end of each day, she would collapse in the front seat of the family car with the air conditioner blowing directly into her face. Sweating all day and getting covered with all sorts of dirt and filth was not her ideal activity, but she never regretted it, not even for a moment.

The thing about serving, she reminded herself, *is if you're doing it right then you can never be sad or go wrong, because true service is losing yourself in the work that needs to be done and focusing on all the great stuff you can do for other people. Stuff that would make those you're serving feel better about themselves, and in return, you end up feeling better about yourself.*

Over the course of the days they were there helping, Evelyn came to truly appreciate the effort she was making. She realized that she was loving the experience and the joy it brought her. It was a life changing experience that she knew she would reflect upon and draw strength from, throughout the remainder of her life because it was such a special moment in time.

Magazine article about service was found in the debris

Near the final day of their vacation of laboring at our house, I was clearing some debris from the living room area. There I uncovered a weathered and debris riddled magazine. When I bent down to pick it up, I noticed that it had flipped open to an article about service and serving your fellow man. It had been rain soaked and covered with debris, then dried in the sun, forever preserving the tornado's "bookmark" to that particular page.

I picked it up and set it aside, thinking how appropriate it was to what we were experiencing in our own lives. However, the big difference is that we were the recipients of the service, rather than the providers.

When the Texans decided that they needed to get back on the road and head for home, I felt like I needed to give them that magazine with the article about service. I felt like they should have it as a reminder of how they had been a shining example of the actions advocated in that article.

We thanked them for stopping by and getting the chance to have them as our friends. They thanked us for letting them serve, assuring us that it was their pleasure. They promised us there was no place else they would have rather been on their vacation.

Instead of bringing home some big mouse eared hats or other theme park treasures, they were leaving with dirt and grime under their nails and embedded into their skin, along with a raggedy magazine with tornado debris sun baked onto it. Instead of souvenirs, the only thing they had to show for their vacation would be sunburns and lots of dirty clothes. And yet, they thanked us!

"Make sure you send me a friend request," Bonita yelled, as they piled into their car."

"I will," Stacey hollered, with us standing by the street waving as they drove away.

As Evelyn moved closer to the vents that were blowing cold air over her face, she thought about all that had happened over the past few days. Even though they had only been there a short time, and the work accomplished was small in comparison to the destruction, the impact she had on improving someone else's life made everything seem so much better.

The funny thing about service, she thought, as the cool air caressed her face, *is that by the end of it, you're the one being thankful for the opportunity to help out. And it brings you a feeling deep inside that nothing else can duplicate!*

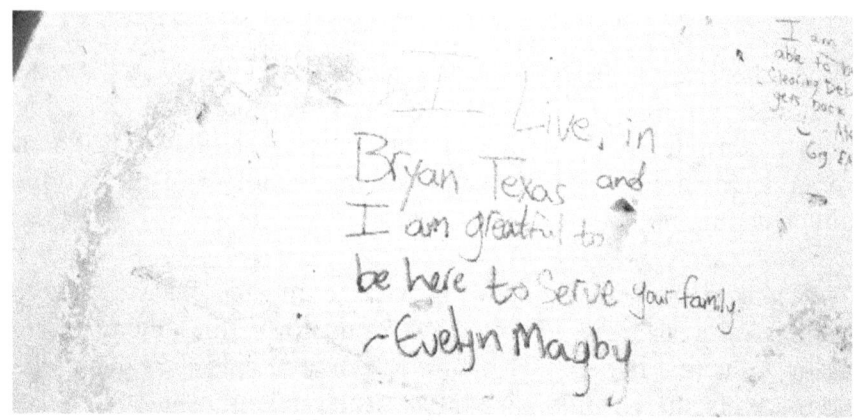

Message on bedroom wall
Photo used with permission: © 2011 by Bonita Magby, All Rights Reserved

On the other side of town, Tawny and Laura continued to work tirelessly each day, filling care packages and then traveling throughout the affected neighborhoods, serving those in need.

Even if they didn't need a care package, everyone needed a smile or words of encouragement. They knew that each day of their service added quality of life to more of God's children and was worthy of their best efforts.

Yes, we need a house, a car, food, clothing, furniture, and a cell phone to function in society, Laura thought, *but the most important things we need are each other. Our relationships with all the people around us are more important than everything else. I could have brought endless bottles of lotions and gifts, but what really helped people more was a hug, a tear, and a smile.*

She knew all too well that the loss of a loved one was a difficult thing to overcome. She wished Brett could be by her side, helping pick up the pieces of her splintered hometown. She longed for his companionship, starting a family, and making plans for the future. Even though that could never be, she took assurance in knowing that her joy with him was greater than any sadness will ever be.

She knew that same realization would strengthen the families whose lives had been devastated by the tornado. She could see it in the eyes of those with whom she had visited, and she knew how grateful they were for their families and loved ones.

The tornado and its aftermath had forever changed her life. *I wish it hadn't destroyed homes,* she lamented, *and I wish with all my heart that it hadn't taken any lives, but it made me have hope for all of us. I now know, without any doubt, the love in this world overpowers any kind of hate. We are powerful people when we have charity in our hearts!"*

What a great joy it was for Tawny to relate the stories of miracles and blessings to her friends and family back in Wyoming. Every person who said, "we took cover in the hall closet" or "we went to the bathroom" or "we ran downstairs" then finished with, "and when it was over, it was the only thing left standing" confirmed to her that God knows us as individuals and has absolute power to protect us, if it is His will.

She had pondered many times upon the repeated stories of the butterflies and butterfly people, who had not only protected many children and others from the storm, but comforted them during and afterwards. This was not only a powerful spiritual message to her, but the confirmation of a real miracle in every sense.

This miracle of God protecting and comforting the children helped her overcome what seemed to be the "unfairness" of the loss of lives. *Even though it is unknown to us why our loved ones are taken*, she reinforced to herself, *God knows. And if we have trust in Him and love Him, it can be a source of comfort, if we allow it.*

She knew that to be true, because she had been comforted as she watched her daughter work through the grief of losing Brett when his death seemed so unfair in every possible way.

However, as Laura had often reminded her, *the joy of having loved someone in our lives, for whatever length of time, outweighs our sorrow. Love is always a miracle and indeed the only thing, that in the end, really matters.*

Messages on wall studs and in the hall coat closet

Meanwhile, about four hundred miles to the southeast, in Germantown, Tennessee, Katie received a call from her friend Alli.

"Hey Katie," she said, "one of the kids dropped out of the mission trip and I got permission to invite you to go with us."

"Isn't that tomorrow?"

"Yes ma'am, we're leaving first thing in the morning on the bus."

Katie felt a rush of anxiety, reasoning that she would have to drop everything to leave on a trip with such short notice. Not only that, she didn't have time to prepare and couldn't afford it. She expressed her concerns to Alli, who assured her the trip had been paid for and she would simply take that person's place in the group.

"I don't know. I don't even know anything about it... all I heard was something mentioned it in history class right before school ended. I'll have to call you back in an hour and let you know."

After she ended the call she went straight to her mother, expressing her concerns and fears.

"I just don't know what to do Mom, it's such short notice and I don't know what I'm getting myself into. Do you think I should go or tell Alli there's just not enough time for me to get ready?"

"Have you prayed about it?" her mother asked, "I'm sure God will tell you what to do."

"You're right Mom, that's what I'll do."

Katie returned to her bedroom and began praying for guidance. She picked up her Bible and began thumbing through it, searching for an answer that would ease her anxiety and fears, giving her the direction she needed.

Her Bible fell open to Romans, chapter eight, where she read, *For you did not receive a spirit that makes you a slave again to fear, but you received a spirit of sonship. And by him we cry, Abba,*

Father. The Spirit himself testifies with our spirit that we are God's children.

She felt her anxiety and fears melt away, knowing that God had given her His answer. It was settled, she would be leaving for Joplin the next day with her friend and their church group.

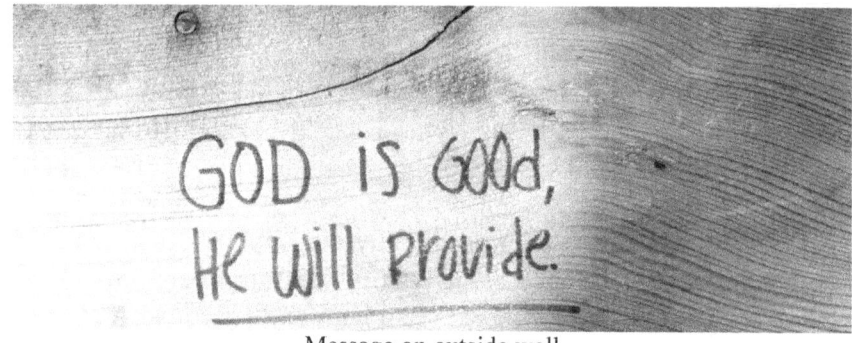

Message on outside wall

She raced into the living room to announce to her parents that she was going on the mission trip to Joplin. Her parents approved of her decision and reinforced their support for her. They were proud that she had chosen to participate in such a worthy cause.

She returned to her room and called Alli to secure her spot on the bus. They were both excited to be able to serve together. They chatted for a few minutes and Katie ended the call so she could start packing her things.

While she packed, she contemplated this unique and unexpected opportunity. During the past year she had several opportunities to register for other trips that would have taken place at this same time over the summer. In fact she had even been accepted to a program that would have taken her on a trip to three European countries, which was something she had always wanted to do. If she had taken any of those other trips, she wouldn't have been able to go with Alli to Joplin.

She remembered her feelings (or lack thereof) when praying about the other trips and opportunities. She knew each time that it just wasn't the right thing to do. She compared that to the answer she had just received, and knew beyond any doubt that it was the right decision to wait. *For some reason*, she thought, *it is God's desire for me to make this journey*.

When she finished packing her things into a large suitcase, she gently placed her Bible in last and zipped it shut. Even though she had no idea what lay ahead of her for the next week, she had a warm, peaceful feeling and the assurance that she would be doing what God had chosen for her.

Back in Joplin and later that evening I received a call from Becky, one of the volunteer leaders from the National Relief Network. I concluded that Becky was from the UK because she had a noticeable british accent. She told me that she was excited to meet me and work with the crews to help us dig out of our mess. She asked if she could meet with me first thing on Monday morning with the rest of the group. I told her that worked well for me and I looked forward to meeting her.

In the early hours of the next morning in a quiet church parking lot, a few adult leaders, Donnie, Beckie Jo, Larry, and Kayra, were making final preparations to board a bus with their group of teenagers and young adults. Other parents and their teenagers were removing suitcases and bags from their cars and loading them onto the bus.

For Ian, this would not be his first such trip, but it would be more personal for him this time. A couple who had attended school with his parents lived in Joplin. Even though they were not directly affected by the tornado, he felt a personal connection in serving the community where family friends lived.

Waiting to board the bus, he thought back to his previous mission trip. He had been a part of the relief effort in Nashville, after the flooding. The memories of the backbreaking work played out vividly in his mind. He and his fellow volunteers had put in many long, hard hours under an unforgivingly hot sun.

Message on a wall stud

A smile slowly covered his face as he recalled the people he had met, whom he had helped, and the spiritual boost that he brought back to Tennessee with him. *It was all worth it*, he thought, thankful to God for giving him a strong work ethic and a strong stature. He was blessed both mentally and physically to provide assistance to others and he enjoyed the hard work.

Ian had grown up living a comfortable life in a quiet, small town.

He had never experienced any hard times or been exposed to much disaster. Mission time was an opportunity to see more of the world and help those in less fortunate circumstances than his own.

Making a mental checklist to be sure he wasn't leaving anything important behind, his mind wandered back to the past year of fund raising activities. All of the money required to make the mission trip to the disaster site had to be raised in its entirety, prior to departing.

Some of the fundraisers included selling hams / boston butts, car washes, luncheons, and the most demanding of all, the metal drive. Collecting scrap metal was a laborious job as much of the scrap metal collected was quite heavy.

"Hey Ian," one of the leaders yelled, "have you got all your stuff loaded?"

"Yes sir," he shouted, as he headed toward the line that was beginning to form at the front of the bus.

Once everyone had boarded the bus, the door closed and mission trip was officially underway. Ian settled into his seat, placing ear buds in his ears, determined to make the drive more pleasurable.

A few seats ahead of him, two friends, Alli and Katie were getting settled in for the long trip ahead. Alli rested her head against the seat, staring out the window, watching her family and friends disappear into the distance as the bus drove away. A tear trickled down her cheek as she contemplated leaving the security of her familiar life behind, for the unknown journey that lay ahead.

It was a bittersweet moment for her. She was excited to be doing the work of the Lord and knew that God approved of her commitment. The theme for this mission trip was "Faith in Action." It was important for her and the rest of the group to be an example of that theme in all that they hoped to do, in helping to ease the suffering of their brothers and sisters in need.

She was a little unsure of what she would do and how she would react once the group actually got their feet on the ground. She was familiar with the destructive force of tornadoes and the havoc they could wreak. She had never been personally involved with any tornadoes, but there was a constant stream of news coverage on TV of the damage in Joplin. She knew in her heart that God would find a way for her to serve and she left it in His hands.

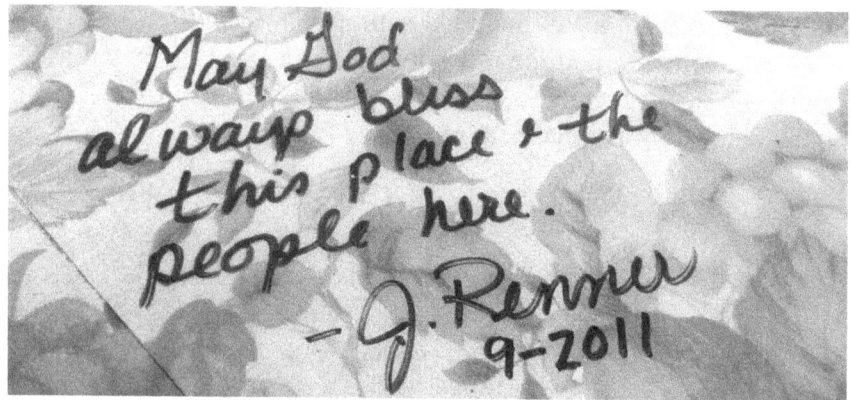

Message on a shelf in the linen closet

Meanwhile, nearly six hundred miles to the northeast in Aurora, Illinois, school was in summer recess for Phil, a drama and music teacher. He, like the rest of the nation, had been following the news coverage of the destruction that had taken place in Joplin and the relief efforts that were underway.

He felt the calling voice of the Good Shepherd to go and tend to His sheep. Because he had the summer off from school, he could cancel some of his private music lessons and take some time to go help his neighbors. *Lori and I could stay with the local church there*, he assured himself, *and lend a helping hand, along with their congregation.*

Lori was Phil's girlfriend, and he was certain that she would also want to go along and help out. As he contemplated making the trip, doubt began to creep into his mind and trouble his spirit. Recently, he had been feeling confused about his faith and at times struggling to remain strong and faithful. His relationship with God just wasn't as strong as he had hoped for and wanted it to be.

His relationship with Lori had been strained for some time and that also troubled him. Something was missing, but he just couldn't put his finger on it. Things just weren't as wonderful and magical as he had hoped they would be and thought they should be.

On top of all that, he thought, almost in despair, *I've got to get the set built over the summer for the high school play.* When he had signed on as the drama teacher, he had no idea that one day he would be in charge of a huge construction project for which he had no carpentry skills or training.

Maybe I should just stay here, he reasoned, *and try to get my life fixed up and headed in the right direction before I try to help others fix their lives. After all, I'm just one person and there will be lots of volunteers, who are probably better qualified than me to help out.*

That evening Phil and Lori made their decision, and put their trust in God. They were committed to going to Joplin to help out wherever God would send them and do whatever was needed. They packed their bags and made the necessary arrangements to be away for a week.

That night Phil lay awake in bed, unable to sleep. Even though he had committed to doing God's will, he was still struggling internally, his heart and soul still racked with doubt and anxiety. After much soul searching, he was still unclear about everything important to him and his future. Eventually his emotional and spiritual struggles wore him out and he drifted off to sleep.

The next day, the drive to Joplin was long and for the most part, quietly uneventful... until they pulled into town. Even though he and Lori had followed the news coverage, they were horrified by what they actually saw when they drove into the path of destruction. What they had seen on the news didn't even begin to capture what they were now witnessing with their own eyes.

Message on a brick of the chimney

"Oh dear Lord," Lori gasped in disbelief, "it's worse than I could have ever imagined. What must it be like for these people?"

"It looks like hell on earth," Phil whispered, as the tried to take in the magnitude of destruction, "I can't even begin to imagine what it must have been like."

He was having a difficult time wrapping his mind around what he was seeing as they drove further into the "red zone" of destruction. His own problems suddenly seemed insignificant as he tried to imagine the suffering that so many people were dealing with at that very moment.

When they finally arrived at the church where they would take up

142

temporary residency, they were greeted by several others who were there to help. They spent some time getting to know the people they would be working with in providing relief to the community. Phil found it therapeutic to his own troubled soul, just being around others who wanted nothing more than to help their neighbors and glorify God.

Later that day, he found himself in a private conversation with two pastors. The conversation eventually led to Phil's troubled spirit and the struggles he had been trying to work through. They counseled and prayed together. By the end of the meeting, he had been provided with a much needed spiritual boost, strengthening and reinforcing his wavering faith and ultimately, his calling.

That evening as assignments were being made for the various relief projects that were being undertaken, much to his surprise, he was assigned to the team in charge of building sheds.

"I don't have any building experience or skills," he said to Howard, another member of the team, "I don't even own a hammer."

"Well, the good thing about it," Howard said, grinning from ear to ear, "is that you won't be able to say that when you leave here!"

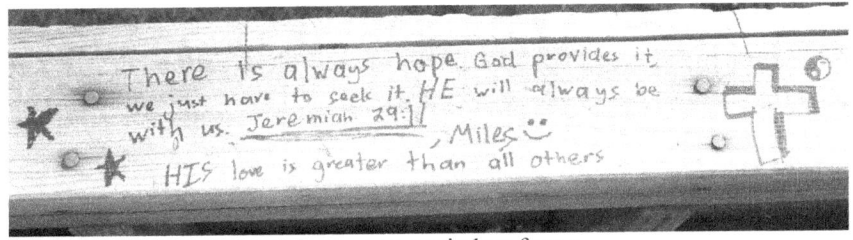

Message on a window frame

His mind quickly flashed back to his previous dilemma... carrying the huge burden of building the entire set for the high school play, and being woefully unprepared for such an undertaking.

The Lord really does work in mysterious ways, he thought, feeling the distinct presence, guidance, and love of God in his life... *surely, the Lord had provided.*

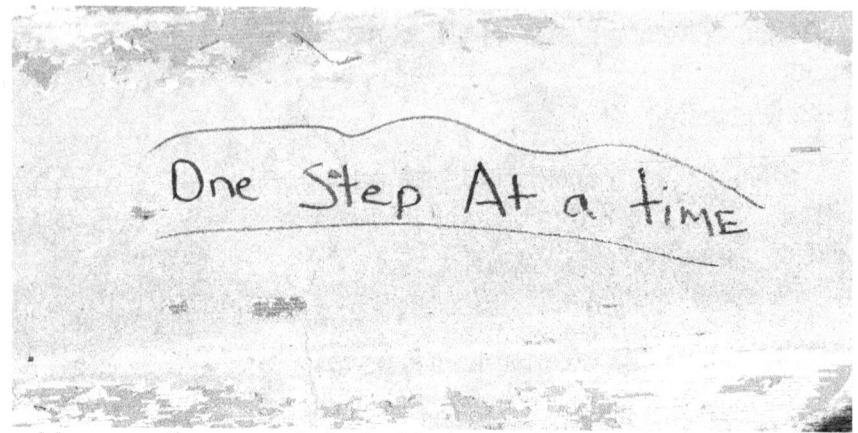

Message on the steps at the back of the house - Photo used with permission:

As the bus from western Tennessee crept into Joplin, it stopped at the edge of town. The weary travelers were anxious to grab a bite to eat and take a few minutes to stretch after the long bus ride.

Once inside, the group filled many of the tables in the restaurant and the air was filled with chatter about the cleanup efforts they were there to facilitate.

A couple of the waiters overheard their conversation and began chatting with the group where Alli was seated.

"How bad is it," someone asked.

"It's unimaginable," one of the waiters said, "until you see for yourself, you just can't imagine how bad it really is."

Retrieving a cell phone from his pocket, the waiter played a video he had taken at ground zero, giving them a visual of what it was really like.

I had no idea it was going to be this bad, Alli thought as she watched the video, *what would I have done if I had to sit through that tornado, not knowing if I would survive or not?*

After they were finished with their meal, the group left the restaurant and boarded the bus. Being a group of mostly teenagers and young adults, the atmosphere was a little loud, energetic, and perhaps a bit rowdy.

Driving onward into the swath of destruction left by the tornado, the bus fell silent. All eyes were fixated out the windows, upon the total devastation of the terrain that surrounded them. The news footage they had seen previously couldn't prepare them for what they now witnessed with their own eyes.

Even the leaders who had experienced many of life's challenges, were shocked and overwhelmed with what they were seeing. Everyone on that bus was gripped with emotion and compassion for the injured bodies, hearts, and souls that were so profoundly affected. Many tears were shed and many silent prayers of thanks were given as the bus made its way slowly through town.

When it came time for *lights out* that night, many of the Tennessee volunteers were struggling with sleep. Mission trip had taken on a whole new meaning for them. The spirit whispered to them, making it known that their purpose was more than just picking up debris. It was about lifting spirits. God would use them as an instrument in His hands to magnify the faint glimmer of the light of hope, that for the people of Joplin, was almost indiscernible at the end of a very, very long tunnel.

Message above the arch between the dining room and living room

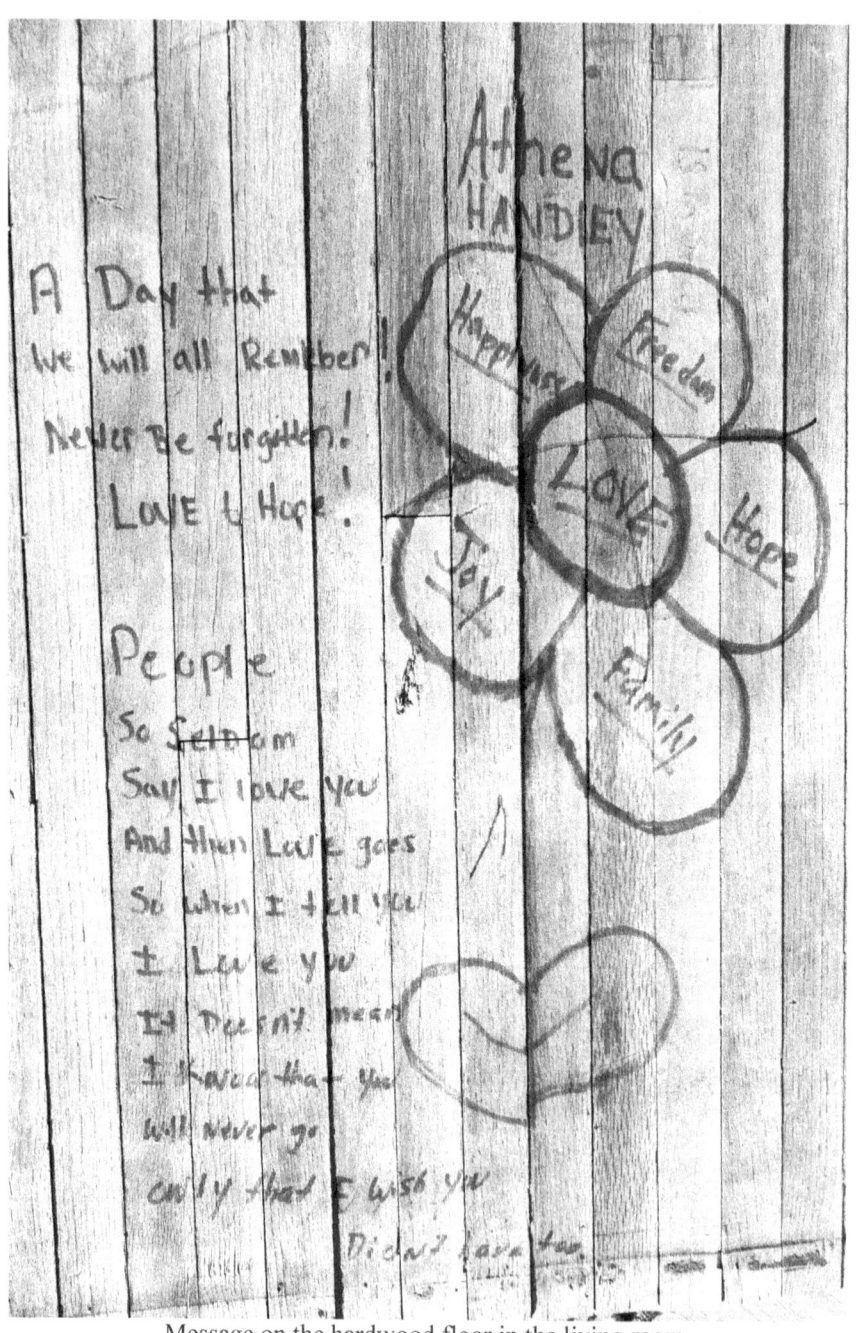

Message on the hardwood floor in the living room
(more color photos, stories & information available at www.jthoh.com)

Chapter 7

The following morning came too early for Stacey and me. We were exhausted, but the crowing of the rooster in my in-law's back yard made sure that we didn't lose any sunlight. I had always enjoyed the fresh eggs we received weekly from my mother-in-law, but today I was thinking more along the lines of freshly fried chicken or perhaps some Szechuan rooster!

After we got ready for the day, we hurried to Carthage to drop Stacey off at work and then I raced over to Joplin. When I got to the house, I was greeted by a very bubbly, charming, and outgoing woman who asked me if I was "Mr. Tim."

"I am, and you must be Becky," I said, shaking her hand.

"Yes," she said, smiling brightly, "and we're glad to be here to help you."

"Yer not from around these here parts, are ya," I asked in my best redneck twang.

"I'm actually from the UK," she said through her fairly thick accent, smiling even broader.

"What brings you all this way from home?"

"I absolutely love doing this, and I love getting to work with so many amazing people and helping all the wonderful people like yourself and the rest of your fine community."

"You have no idea how glad I am that you came here to help us."

"It really is my pleasure... we're all very happy to be here!"

She then introduced me to one of her assistants, CJ, a young college student, who had given up her summer vacation to help in the tornado cleanup, assigned as one of the NRN group leaders.

"It's nice to meet you," she said, shaking my hand, "I'm glad to be here and help out. Your house has become famous."

"How's that?"

"It's all over the news and on the internet... it's gone viral. It has a great message and is giving hope to a lot of people."

"Wow, that's really cool, I was hoping that it would inspire others."

"It definitely has!"

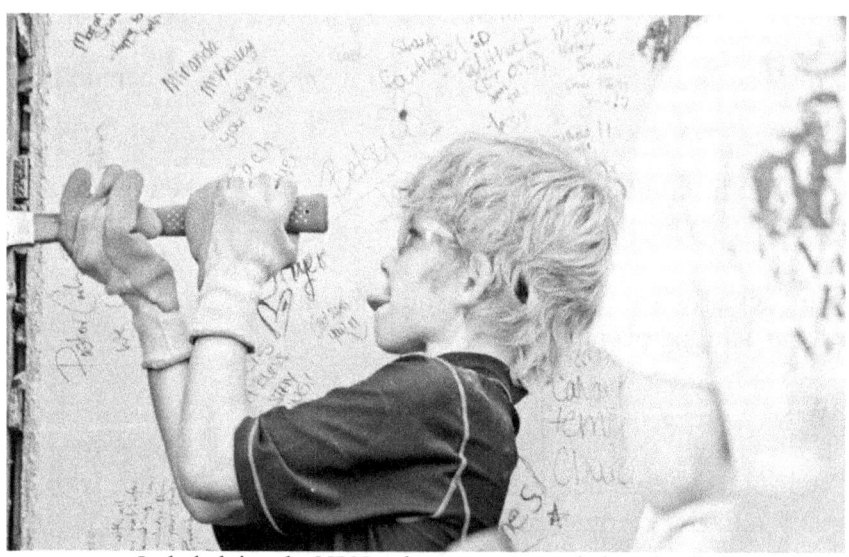

Jack, helping the NRN volunteers remove lath and nails

I was glad to hear that our house was becoming recognized around the country. I wasn't aware of the notoriety it had gained on the world wide web, because we hadn't had access to the internet since the tornado hit. We worked all day long, then traveled to Arkansas at night, where the only internet access my in-laws had was a slow dial-up connection. It was so slow, you could watch text being printed, a few words at a time on the screen.

Becky turned to the volunteers, a large group of mostly teenagers, young adults, and a handful of leaders. They were all dressed in bright, sparkling clean yellow t-shirts with the NRN logo printed on the back. They were adorned with hats, gloves, safety goggles, and most of them clutching various tools such as rakes, shovels, brooms, etc. Absent a couple of flaming torches, they could have passed for a group of medieval villagers who were trying to chase an ogre back to the swamp.

She told them I was going to address the group and say a few words. I was a little taken aback and hadn't expected that I would be speaking. They say more people are afraid of public speaking than death. It just so happens, I'm one of those people. All eyes were fixed on me and I was starting to get a little nervous.

With a bit of hesitation I said, "when the tornado hit, we only had two choices concerning it... upstairs or downstairs. That was the extent of our choices. We didn't have a choice to be here or not, we were stuck here. But each of you had a choice. Each of you gave up a week of your life to come here and dig through this wreckage and debris. And for that, we are forever grateful and you are our heroes. We love you and the community loves you. Thank you, and God bless each of you."

At that point everyone in the group either shook my hand or gave me a hug, assuring me they were glad to be here and help out. It turns out that "help" would be an huge understatement.

The leaders asked where I wanted them to start and what exactly needed to be done. We walked through the house and around the property to get an idea of what needed to be done and how best to proceed. I told them that I wanted to leave the walls intact, where I had spray painted messages and where others were written.

"I'm hoping to be able to rebuild here," I told them, "for the most part, the foundation is still pretty sound and what remains of the framework of the structure is also pretty sound. I'll have to add some walls, put on a roof and then I can start finishing the inside."

With that in mind, we decided to start moving the debris from the property to the curb where the Army Corp of Engineers crews would pick it up and haul it off to the landfill. Another team would begin taking down all the lath and plaster that had been damaged and needed to be removed so that sheetrock could be added later.

One bathroom wall needed to come down and the cast iron tub inside needed to come out. There was the refrigerator / freezer and gas stove that needed to be hauled to the curb, along with the chimney that had fallen into the dining room. There was electrical wire and metal wire sheathing that needed to be cut and removed.

The NRN volunteers throwing a bathroom wall out of the house

I told the group about my daughter next door losing her wedding set and only finding the wedding band thus far, and to be on the lookout for the needle in the haystack that was the engagement ring. I told them about my USB drive that was missing, and whoever found it would be my best friend forever.

One of the adult leaders, Donnie, had brought his young son, Cameron, with him.

That is so cool, I thought, *teaching his boy about the value of hard work and serving others at such a young age!*

Cameron wasn't big enough or strong enough to swing a sledge hammer or haul off large pieces of wood or other building materials. He was however, "the little engine that could!" What he lacked in brute strength, he overcame with enthusiasm.

Even though all our plants, bushes and trees had been pulverized by the twister, because of the deluge of rain we had received some of them started coming up from the roots and began flourishing again. Becky thought it would be a great idea to take the plants out of the ground before they got trampled by the group and put them in pots so they could be transplanted later. It was at that time that Cameron became the official groundskeeper!

He worked tirelessly in digging up various plants in the yard and potted them with potting soil in various pots that Becky had purchased. After he dug them up and potted them I would take them back to my in-law's place. There, Dianne would keep them watered until they could be transplanted.

Because this group of volunteers was going to be there from Monday through Friday, it lent itself to getting to know each other a little better. That was one of the most enjoyable things about this group, getting to know them and them getting to know us. They were not just people with tools and safety goggles, and we were more than just the former occupants of the house.

Most of the group, especially the youth, wanted to know the details of the tornado, our family and how it affected us. As a result, I was able to give many tours and answer lots of questions, which helped put things into perspective for them.

During this time, a friend, Ruby, kept asking me if we needed help. I kept telling her no, that we had it under control with the help of a large volunteer group.

She didn't give up, she just kept asking and asking.

"You're not going to quit asking me, are you?"

"No, I'm not... so when should I show up at your house?"

"We start at nine o'clock in the morning."

"Can I bring people with me?"

How awesome is that, someone wants to come and spend the day with you in the 100+ degree heat (probably closer to 115 degrees when you consider the heat index), digging through nasty tornado debris and sludge. And if that wasn't amazing enough all by itself, she wants to bring her friends along!

Digging through nasty tornado debris and sludge
Photo used with permission: © 2011 by Cathy Giron, All Rights Reserved

The sun rose higher and the temperature climbed right along with it, but the volunteers continued to work tirelessly. On the other hand, I was getting a little worn out hauling junk from the basement to the alley.

Just then, a pickup truck stopped in the street and much to my relief a man climbed out, walking towards me. This gave me an opportunity to take a much needed breather. I tossed the trash I had hauled out of the basement into a pile and started walking toward him to see what he wanted.

"Is this yours," he asked, pointing to our house.

"It is," I said.

"My name is Patrick," he said, reaching into his shirt pocket, retrieving a business card and handing it to me. "I'm with the Joplin Convention and Visitors Bureau."

"Nice to meet you."

"Are you planning on rebuilding?"

"We're hoping to. What's still standing is in pretty good shape, so we may just use what's left as the starting point."

"If you decide not to rebuild or you want to remove that wall," he continued, pointing to the south wall that had the message of love to the volunteers painted on it, "we would like to have it to put in a museum that the city is planning to build, in remembrance of the events surrounding the tornado."

"That would be great. If we decide to remove that wall for any reason, I will definitely give you a call."

We shook hands and he wished me good luck with the cleanup and rebuilding. I tucked his business card into my wallet. Because we were still living out-of-pocket, I knew the only place I might not lose a business card would be in my wallet.

CJ must be right, I thought, reflecting on what she had said previously, *the city wants to put that wall in a museum*.

What happened over the next four days is what I imagine it must be like to witness a swarm of locusts descending upon fertile croplands, except in reverse. If I hadn't personally witnessed it I may not have believed the transformation that took place on our property was done entirely by hand, with nothing more than determination and a few hand tools.

The NRN volunteers moved tons of debris to the alley and curb

The group brought in large tarps that they piled full of debris. Once the debris tarp was full, several of them would drag it to the curb or alley and turn it over, emptying the contents for the trucks to pick up. They had divided into smaller groups, each attacking different challenges of getting the house moved to the curb.

I went back into the bedroom where I continued to inch my way through the debris on my hands and knees, hoping to find my USB drive. While that seemed tedious, it was nothing, compared to what some of the volunteers were doing. Many of them were on their hands and knees inching their way through a debris pile that stretched the entire length of our house, up to twelve feet wide.

As you might expect, the older boys in the group focused on the heavy demolition tasks. They were like miniature wrecking balls, utilizing sledge hammers, log splitting mauls, hammers, and pry bars. Anything that wasn't not structurally sound was reduced to kindling in very short order.

In the basement, there was a big cabinet and countertop from when the house had originally been built. It was made of solid wood (i.e. not particle board) with lots of doors and drawers. It was about twelve feet long. I had used it for a work bench and tool storage in my workshop area.

It needed to come out of the basement, taken to the curb and hauled off to the landfill. It was waterlogged and way too heavy to be carried out by hand. When it came time to remove it, I had no difficulty finding volunteers to break it apart into manageable pieces that could be easily carried out of the basement.

Along the way, there were some cuts and scrapes and the occasional bump on the head, but by and large, no serious injuries. And the good news was that anyone who got a cut or stepped on a rusty nail, the tetanus shot booth was just across the street.

This group was also kind enough to save all the hardwood and put it in the crawl space, down in the basement, so that it could be restored and reused when the house was rebuilt. They also painstakingly removed the mortar from the loose bricks that hadn't been broken and neatly piled them on the front porch area so they could be used on the house later.

Somebody had also gathered all the window counterweights into a neat pile on the ground. Window counterweights were used in construction of older homes to keep the windows open. They were attached to a rope that ran through a pulley at the top of the window frame and down inside a pocket on both sides of the window. There were different sizes used to match the weight of the window with which they were being used.

Window counterweight (center) attached to a rope

For example, if you had a ten pound window, it would take two counterweights that weighed five pounds each, one on either side of the window. When properly attached, the window could be raised to any height and stay in place because the counterweights kept the window equally balanced.

In modern construction, most windows are much lighter and are typically held in place via clips, friction, or springs, negating the need for counterweights.

The window counterweights used in the construction of the homes in our neighborhoods were about twelve to eighteen inches long,

156

about one and a half to two inches thick, made of solid iron and were quite heavy. Imagine the damage they could do, spinning around a tornado at well over two hundred miles per hour!

Kayra asked me if I minded if she took one of the counterweights back home with her. Because the group had relied on collecting scrap metal as a fund raiser, she thought it would be symbolic of their efforts and something to remind her of their trip to Joplin.

"Take all you want," I told her, "and some bricks if you'd like."

"If you don't mind," she continued, "I'd like to have a couple of the brass hinges off one of the doors."

"You can take anything you want; hinges, counterweights, doors, the stove, refrigerator, or anything else for that matter."

She laughed and told me she just wanted something really simple to remind her of this year's mission trip. I reminded her not to forget the scrapes, cuts, and bumps they would be taking back along with the tetanus shots many of them had received.

"Don't forget the iron you're getting" I joked, "from all those rusty nails you stepped on that may be with you the rest of your life!"

The work continued smoothly and every day was noticeably better than the previous day... not just a little, but a lot. At the end of each day, the group would gather together, put away all the tools, thank me again, and head across the street for the bus waiting to take them away until the next day.

By their second day on the job, I had picked through every piece of debris in our bedroom. Much to my dismay, I did not find the USB drive that had all my important computer files on it. I was disheartened by that, because I had spent several years working on the various files it contained.

Worse yet, Stacey's book files were now gone with the wind. They would already be at the publisher, running through the printing press, had it not been for the tornado.

Still, I had to count my many other blessings. Losing these files wasn't the end of the world, and besides, what had once been created could be recreated... it was just going to take a lot of time and effort. It was becoming evident that not only did we lose lots of material possessions, we were also losing time... time that could never be replaced.

Now that I was no longer stuck in the bedroom, I could spend more time with the group in the various locations they were working. As we were removing the lath and plaster from the middle bedroom, I noticed that a robin had built a nest at the top of the wall, above the window frame. I suppose the robins chose this spot, because there were no trees with branches or leaves in the vicinity.

Robins built a nest above the window frame in Abby's bedroom

I made sure to notify the others in the group to not disturb the nest. Even though we had lost our home, there was no reason that the robins should lose theirs.

The volunteers were often rotated from working on site of a residential lot to working in one of the relief centers. Work in the relief centers could mean serving hot meals and providing cold drinks, helping with packaged food distribution, or assisting with clothing and other personal items.

Rotating through the various assignments and stations allowed them to experience different aspects of the suffering and needs of the community. Helping with the cleanup of a home was mostly hot and demanding work. Serving food was providing immediate relief to those working outside. Providing clothing and other personal items was helping to put clothes on people's backs.

Tori, another Tennessee volunteer had been assigned to working in a food and clothing distribution center. After breakfast, she went to the center, anxious to help. As she walked through the relief center amongst the people who had come for help, she had to fight back the tears. For many, all they had was the clothes on their backs and the memories of what once was.

These people were standing in the middle of stacks of canned and boxed goods, but none of them even had cupboards. Tori felt helpless and wished there was more that she could do. She wished that somehow she could wash away the pain and the hurt that was so visible on the faces and in the voices of so many. She felt guilty that her own life was not broken and battered.

And then something changed all that. A tall, slender woman with flowing, dark hair and a weathered complexion approached her and struck up a conversation. From her mannerisms to the tone of her voice, Tori could tell that this stranger didn't have a mean bone in her body. She exuded genuine gratitude, joy, and peace.

"How are you," Tori asked.

"I'm doing well. I survived without any injuries and I'm here talking to you," the woman replied confidently.

She went on to share her story. She told of how she had lost everything... her home, car, clothes, and other personal items... all of it gone.

"The only things I didn't lose are the clothes on my back, but that's okay. What really matters is that I'm alive and all my friends and family are alive and safe."

NRN volunteers working in a thrift center

Tori stood motionless and speechless listening intently to every word, trying to imagine what it must be like to be in this woman's shoes. *How can she be so positive*, she asked herself, *when she has lost so much?*

"I cried a lot that first day, but now I thank God constantly, because he continues to bless me. Everything I have and every day I'm alive is a gift from above," she said, lifting her eyes upward.

That moment would forever change Tori's life. Here was a woman whose life had been shattered into many pieces that were forever lost to her. But her faith in God had gathered and mended the most important pieces... her heart and soul.

She didn't grieve for what had been taken away and those things which she no longer had. Instead, she was full of life, love, and gratitude for what she did have... her precious gifts from God.

The only person who truly has nothing, Tori concluded, *is the person who has no faith. With faith, you have treasures beyond measure.*

From that day forward, it became easier for her to see the many miracles, both big and small that occurred not only in the lives of others, but in her own life as well.

In the end it doesn't matter whether we have a home or other possessions, Tori determined, *it's that we get to stay and live for God while we have the chance. We are in the safety of God's hands, even though at times it may seem otherwise.*

The beginning of the third day of work with the Tennessee volunteers started out with assignments being given and a reminder to drink lots of water to stay hydrated. Every morning they brought coolers full of iced down drinks and boxes of snacks. Because there were no trees, it was difficult to find a way to get out of the blistering hot sun, making proper hydration essential.

I grabbed a claw hammer and began helping a group tear down the lath and plaster off some of the walls. Plaster dust filled the air and covered every inch of bodies and clothing on those working in the area. When the plaster dust mixed with sweat, it stuck like glue and then hardened when it dried. It gave new meaning to having a "facial mask."

The worst part of removing the lath is that each piece was held to the studs by several nails. When you removed a piece and it fell to the floor, it created an immediate hazard of stepping on rusty nails.

Later that morning, Adam stopped by and came walking up the back steps. When I saw him out of the corner of my eye, I stopped what I was doing and pulling my particle mask down under my chin, stepped aside to talk to him.

"What brings you here?"

"I thought I'd look for Tiffany's engagement ring."

"Are you still holding out hope for that?"

"Yeah, but more importantly, it gives me the chance to bother you while I'm here!"

"Well, at least you're honest about it... there are some masks and gloves on the ledge under the deck. Good luck finding the ring, but don't hold your breath."

Adam donned a mask and gloves and walked around the south side of the house, where a group was sifting through the debris and hauling it off to the alley. He dropped to his hands and knees and began inching through the debris with the others.

I pulled my mask up on my face and went back to pulling the lath and plaster down.

It probably wasn't more than an hour later when I heard a bunch of commotion from the south side of the house. Within seconds, someone came running up the stairs shouting, "Mr. Tim, they found it... Cathy found your daughter's engagement ring!"

By this time everyone had stopped working and were rushing to the side of the house. There stood Cathy with her mask down, gloves off, cradling a gold, diamond ring gently in her hand.

162

Against all odds, Cathy finds Tiffany's engagement ring in the debris

"I almost don't believe it," she said, "but I found it!"

I walked over to her so I could get a closer look.

"That's amazing," I said, still surprised to see it in her hand, "I figured that ring was gone for good. Where's Adam?"

"He's on the phone, down the street."

I looked down the street and sure enough, there he was with his cell phone pressed to his head, making gestures and motions with his free hand.

"So he doesn't know you found it?"

"No, he got the phone call before I found it."

"Hmmm... you found it buried on my property, so I have to believe that technically the ring is mine," I said jokingly, "you know, finders keepers, losers weepers!"

I knew he and Tiffany would be excited, but I wanted to make it a really memorable experience for them and the group. I swore the volunteers to silence and told them I was going to tell the pilgrims that someone had been injured on their lot, to get Tiffany to come over immediately and then we could reveal the ring to her.

Adam reveals the ring to Tiffany

I called Tiffany and told her that someone had been injured on their lot and she needed to hurry over to the house. She was worried and told me she was on her way.

I met Adam as he was walking back up the street. I told him the same story. Both he and Tiffany were now a little shaken up, thinking someone had been hurt.

Before Tiffany got there, one of the group caved in and told Adam that nobody was hurt and that Cathy had found the ring. Adam was both relieved and ecstatic, about there being no injury and Cathy finding the ring.

When Tiffany arrived, she was visibly upset. I was certain that she would be happy when she learned that nobody had been injured. She would be catapulted from happy to overjoyed when she learned that her ring had been found.

Adam took her by the hand, walking toward the spot where Cathy found the ring. He told her not to worry about anyone being hurt. He then dropped down on one knee and revealed the ring, sliding it back on her finger. She was clearly thrilled!

All of the group began to clap and cheer, many of the women wiping tears from their eyes. Tiffany and Adam both hugged Cathy and thanked her for working so hard to find her ring. The odds of finding that ring under those conditions and circumstances seemed pretty unlikely. But that just goes to show you that miracles can come in all shapes and sizes.

For me, that was a big deal. Finding the ring was good, but the great joy and morale boost it gave the group was wonderful. Not only did they find a needle in the haystack, but more importantly, they found a silver lining in a really big, gray cloud.

In the middle of that feel good moment, my attention was quickly diverted to a woman who came walking through the alley, offering popsicles that were still frozen!

Tiffany had brought my granddaughters with her, so Grace and I shared a popsicle out in the back yard, near where we normally would have been picking various types of berries. Sharing that icy cold popsicle could never take the place of picking and eating fresh berries, but under the circumstances, it was probably as close as we would ever get any time soon.

Going back to work and plodding along in the cleanup efforts, I was surprised to see Dan returning to the house.

"Hey Dan, how are you?" I asked.

"I'm fine, thanks. I was talking to my wife who is down here on a reporting assignment. I told her about your house and she wants to come by and see it. If it's okay with you, she might want to do a story on it and maybe interview you."

"Sure, that won't be a problem. I'm here all the time, and if I'm not here, I'm across the street getting something to eat or drink."

He thanked me, wished me a good day and was soon back in his car, driving down the street.

Grace and I enjoying a popsicle together
(more color photos, stories & information available at www.jthoh.com)

Chapter 8

At the beginning of the fourth day with the Tennessee volunteers, it appeared that the remainder of the work would certainly be completed by the end of the day. There was a feeling of great satisfaction and accomplishment that I shared with the group.

I met with Larry and Kayra to go over the list of things that still needed to be finished by the end of the day.

"We're having a barbeque over at the Salvation Army tent tonight, Kayra said, "for you and your family and any friends you want to invite."

"Seriously?" I asked, somewhat surprised.

"We brought several coolers full of food that we're going to cook up tonight," Larry added, "it will be our farewell dinner of thanks."

I sat there for a few moments trying to take in what they had just said. They had worked all year long with their youth to raise money, to drive here so they could spend a week of their summer vacation helping me dig through rubble and literally move a house to the curb by hand. And if that weren't enough, they wanted to spend their last evening here cooking dinner over a hot grill for our family and friends!

"Are you sure you want to do all that after you've done all this?" I asked, pointing to the mountains of building materials, appliances, debris and other things that had been moved to the curb.

"That's exactly what we want to do," Larry said.

"This has been a great blessing for all of us," Kayra insisted, "and we want to do this to thank you for letting us come and serve your family and the community."

"I wouldn't miss it for the world," I said, "I'll round up the family and some friends and we will definitely be there."

The remainder of the day was marked with a more uplifted spirit amongst the group. There was more horseplay between the youth and everyone was more relaxed and casual. By the end of the day, what had once been the scene of chaotic destruction had been returned to a normal looking yard. In fact, it was the first lot in the area that had been completely cleared down to the lawn.

I knew that they must have been feeling a great sense of victory, having overcome such an enormous task. In my mind, I imagined that feeling as being somewhat similar to what Julius Caesar often wrote, "veni, vidi, vici" or translated from Latin, "I came, I saw, I conquered!"

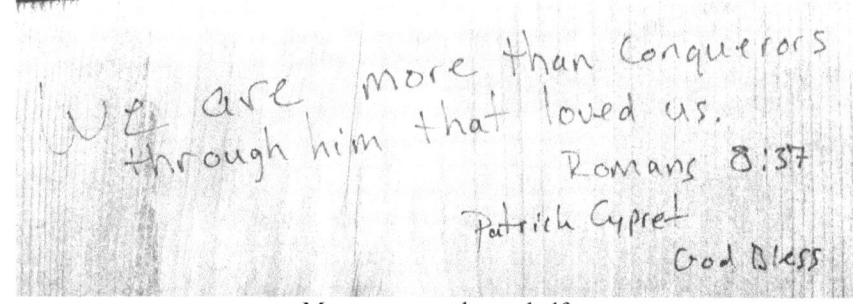

Message on a closet shelf

How many other volunteers who would serve here, I wondered, *would leave with this same satisfaction, gratification, and sense of accomplishment?* Those who came to help us would not return as heroes, conquerors, or victors to their homes at the end of their time in Joplin. But to me, they were nothing less than a glorious, conquering army who marched into town, victoriously drove out the enemy and restored our community, leaving an ensign of hope and love scribbled on the broken walls of our house!

That evening, after picking up Stacey from work, we returned to the Salvation Army relief center. It was relatively quiet as the only

168

people there were the Tennessee volunteers along with our family and friends. Music from a boombox played in the background. The aroma of a variety of charcoal grilled meats wafted through the gently stirring, hot, humid air.

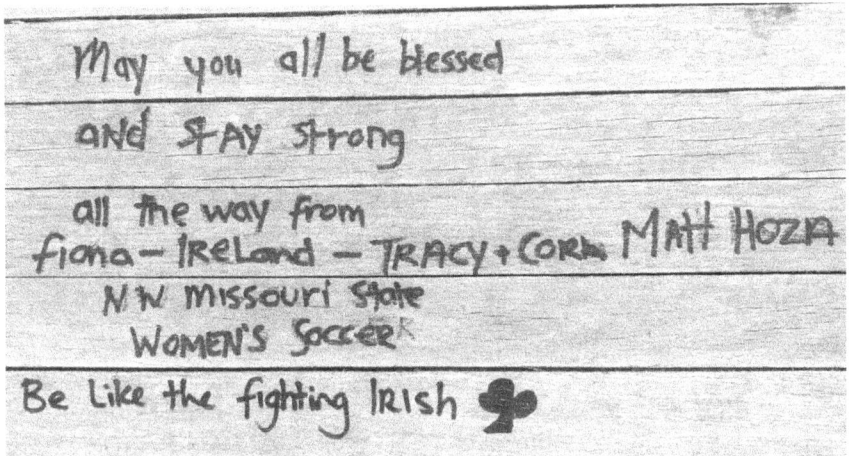
Message on hardwood floor

The group was in a celebratory mood, relaxed, casual, laughing, and enjoying themselves. I made my way around to the various tables, trying to thank everyone for making such a huge sacrifice for my family and the community. Each and every one of them thanked me again.

We finally made our way to the serving line. There were pans full of perfectly grilled meats, side dishes, chips, and coolers full of ice cold drinks. I loaded up my plate and enjoyed a delicious, relaxing meal with family and friends.

Before long, it was time to leave for Arkansas and bid farewell to our new friends. Stacey and I walked over to the adult leaders who had gathered near the front of the tent. They told me they had something to give me before they returned home.

They reached inside a bag and pulled out two t-shirts. The first was an NRN t-shirt with their signatures written on it. The other bore an emblem of a cross with a banner wrapped around it that proclaimed their mission statement of "Faith In Action."

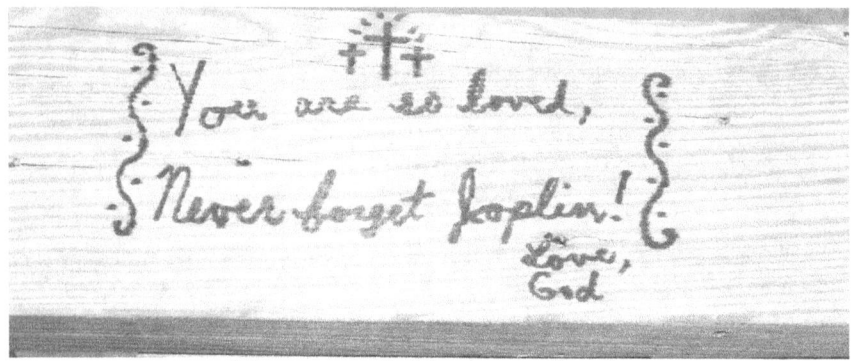

Message on a 2x4 between wall studs

They pulled out two gift cards from the bag and handed one to us and the other to the pilgrims. I was amazed at everything this group had done for us and then they give us gifts after all of that! We thanked them again and said our good-byes.

It was a sentimental ending as we steered the rental car south and drove away from the tent. We were the recipients of a tremendous amount of goodwill and the true love of Christ, expressed in so many different ways. The group would be leaving the next day and I was sad to see them go. However, I knew they were happy to be going back home to reunite with their family and friends.

On Friday morning, they were loading onto the bus, looking forward to a relaxing day they would spend at a water recreation area, floating down a winding river on inner tubes, rubber rafts, and kayaks. It would be a welcomed relief after the past four days of grueling work. There would be no tornado debris, no rusty nails, no plaster dust... just lots of water, shade, and relaxing fun.

As the group settled in and the bus began to pull away, with Joplin disappearing behind them, some of the group began to reflect upon their 2011 mission trip that was now behind them.

Tears began to well up in Alli's eyes. *This mission trip has really changed me*, she thought, *and out of all of them I've been on, this has been my favorite.*

As the bus rolled further away, she wished they could have stayed longer. Even though the work was terribly hot, humid, smelly, dirty, and wore a person out in the first hour, she had fun during the past week. Many people might have challenged her use of the word, "fun," but that's what it was to her.

As Joplin disappeared from sight, she was glad that she had the opportunity to help so many others, both on site and at the various relief centers. She knew that she had done all she could do to help make a difference in the lives of others and in some small way, bring hope to their lives in the days, weeks, and months ahead.

Next to her, Katie sat in silent meditation. She marveled at how God had taken care of all the details and even the money that made it possible for her to go on the mission trip. He had taught her to be humble and put all of her fears to rest and just trust in Him. *He will never put you through anything,* she reassured herself, *that you can't handle with His help.*

Message on window header

She wiped away a tear from her eye and her heart ached to be leaving the people behind that she had genuinely come to love. She was amazed at the incredible hope and optimism of the city and its residents. They were an inspiration to her and she would always treasure the time she was able to spend with them. She now knew why God had chosen this trip for her.

A few rows back, Ian had settled into his seat with his ear buds firmly in place, enjoying the music that brought him comfort and made the trip more pleasant. He too, contemplated the events of the past week. He was proud of the work that he and the group had accomplished. He felt the reassurance of God's approval of their efforts.

It's all about loving your neighbor, he thought, *and then doing something more than just thinking about it. It's more than just sending money to help in a disaster or some other cause. That's all good, but if people stop there, they are cheating themselves of the experience of meeting people in need, face to face, and witnessing the positive changes that take place in their lives.*

Message on outside wall

Tori sat on the other side of the bus, listening to the chatter around her. She was looking forward to a day of fun and relaxation. She was more appreciative of the many blessings in her life than ever before. She remembered the woman who had lost everything but was so full of life. The stranger had brought a miracle into her life. Tori made a commitment to herself and God that she would never lose sight of what is important in life, and always be grateful for everything she had, especially life itself.

Meanwhile, nearly eleven hundred miles to the Northeast, in Toronto, Canada, Jason sat with his staff going over the production details of their upcoming music video. They had recently been shooting video in the southern United States, of the flooding in Tennessee and the tornado in Alabama. The decision was made to go to Joplin soon for more footage to include in the video.

The following day, I returned to the house to do some routine chores that still needed attention. There was lots of sweeping to do, raking the smaller debris out of the yard, etc. There were still things that remained in the basement that needed to be moved out and the basement cleaned up. Eventually, the grass would need to be mowed and trimmed around the house.

I noticed a news vehicle pulling up in the street with another car behind it, which I recognized to be Dan's.

That must be Sloane, I thought, as a young woman emerged from the news vehicle, walking in my direction. Dan got out of his car, grabbed his camera and began taking pictures of the progress being made in the neighborhood since he'd last been there.

"You must be Tim," she said as I met her in the street.

"And you must be Sloane... it's nice to meet you."

Making our way to the house, we had a casual conversation about the tornado, the house, and our story. She asked about the messages I had originally spray painted on the walls.

"I'm really interested in seeing the messages that have been left by others. Do you mind if I look around?"

"Not at all."

She walked along the walls, reading some of the messages left by various volunteers. She paused for a moment.

"Do you have a favorite one?"

"I do," I said, walking to the end of the green wall and pointing, "this one here."

"Can you read it to me?"

"Every hammer swung, every nail pulled, every cut and scrape received, every brick hauled and every trash bucket dumped - you are worth it. And we'd do it again. Liv, Memphis Tennessee."

"Wow, that's amazing!"

Messages on bedroom wall

"It truly is, and to me that's the real story of this tragedy. It's not about the destructive power of the tornado or the statistics surrounding it. It's really about the volunteers and the love they have for us and their willingness to be so selfless in helping and serving their fellow man."

"The messages written on these walls are really uplifting and inspirational," she said, "they're very moving."

Message on wooden wall

"They are, and from all the volunteers who have come by, I can honestly tell you that the messages on these walls resonate the heart, soul, and voice of everyone I've met. And most of them are not written specifically to me and my family, but rather to the people of Joplin and all who are suffering."

She continued to wander through the house, reading the messages, asking about our experience of riding out the tornado, and the story behind the furniture being placed back in the house.

"Originally I put the furniture back in the house so the volunteers would have a clean place to eat lunch or take a break. I put the children's things in the bedroom area later so people passing by might not only see the destruction, but maybe reflect upon the people whose lives were affected in each home."

Once her film crew had set up their equipment, she interviewed me for the news segment she was working on. When the interview was over, she thanked me and wished me and my family good luck in the recovery process.

"What's your email address," she asked, pulling a pen and piece of paper from her pocket.

She scribbled my email address down and then another, tearing away the bottom portion of the paper.

"Here's my email," she said, handing me the torn piece of paper, "let's keep in touch."

Dan was just returning from taking pictures of the surrounding neighborhood. He and Sloane made arrangements to meet up at the end of the day, climbed into their vehicles and drove away.

Sloane's news segment - Photo used with permission:

Later that evening, Stacey and I went over to Tim and Aly's house so we could view the news segment on the station's website. One of the anchors started out by saying that, "over forty thousand volunteers have made their way through Joplin and one homeowner has found a way to pay it back."

The camera then cut to Sloane's field report, where she called the house an "oasis of hope." Throughout her piece the camera panned from one message to another that had been written on what she called, "the wall of hope."

A few days later, I was at the house raking some smaller debris out of the yard when Dan pulled up. He had come to deliver two 8x10 pictures that he had taken before.

The pictures were amazing. They captured in a way that words can't describe, the emotion, tragedy, and fury of the disaster in a very personal way for Stacey and me. I was very glad that we had accepted the offer to let him take the pictures.

Dan was interested in knowing how things had been going since he last saw us. I updated him on what we had accomplished and what still needed to be done. While we stood there chatting in the back yard I noticed a man riding a bicycle, turning the corner at the end of the street. As he approached us I could see that he was somewhat disheveled in his appearance.

"Hey, I like what you've done with your house," he yelled, waiving his hand to get our attention.

"Thanks," I shouted back, giving him the thumbs-up.

His comment was one that I had already heard a few times before, but it was still appropriate. Upon reaching us he stopped his bicycle and leaned over onto one foot.

"No," he insisted, "I *really* like what you've done with it, the furniture looks nice up there."

"Thanks, I'm glad you like it."

"I'm helping my friend over on Byers avenue," he said, turning and pointing back in the direction from which he had come, "he didn't have insurance, so I'm going to help him rebuild. I'm just headed over to the Salvation Army to get some lunch."

I wished him luck with the rebuilding effort that he was undertaking, trying to imagine what his lot in life was that made him think that my beat-up furniture sitting on a battered and beaten wreck of a house was somehow pleasing to him.

Furniture sitting in the living room

Standing beside our splintered house, not knowing what the future held for us, I was once again reminded just how blessed and fortunate my family and I really were. Not only were we alive and well, but we still had furniture that by some standards was in really good condition.

Later that day, on the other side of town, Phil and Lori were preparing to leave Joplin, having served the community well. They made their way around the church and said their good-byes to all the new friends they had made. They felt like they had accomplished a lot of good and were anxious to share their experiences with their friends and family back home.

On their way out of town they decided to take a tour of the areas

178

where they hadn't worked. They were anxious to see how much progress had been made around town. While they were making their way around the hardest hit areas, crisscrossing the various neighborhoods, Phil noticed a neon green wall a few streets over.

"Look at that," he said to Lori, "there are messages on the walls of that house. Let's go take a closer look."

When they pulled up to the house, they could see that there were messages written all over the walls. They were intrigued by the messages and the furniture that remained in the house. They got out of their car and walked up to take a closer look.

As they wandered through the house reading the messages that had been left behind by other volunteers, they were flooded with emotions. A feeling of overwhelming peace filled Phil's heart and soul like he had never felt before.

And then, like a roller coaster, he had a surge of sadness followed by hope and many other emotions. The grab bag of emotions came and went as he contemplated the tragedy and damage everywhere he looked, in stark contrast to the messages of love and inspiration that had been left by others.

Message next to hole in the living room wall - Photo used with permission:

Standing there on an island of serenity amidst a sea of destruction, his eyes were drawn to a hole in the plaster of one of the remaining walls. A very distinct thought came to his mind that, *God will fill the hole with something new and different.*

He looked around and saw some markers inside a broken "Winnie the Pooh" coffee cup. He grabbed a marker and began writing near the hole in the wall, "God fills all holes." *He seems to know what you need*, he thought, *and then turns your life around and upside down if necessary, so that you can see things His way.*

Phil could feel that this was a special place where he was standing. A place where people could come together in one place and pray... and contemplate... and write their feelings... and just let go emotionally. He could feel that God was looking at him and accepted him for who he was and the direction in which his life was headed.

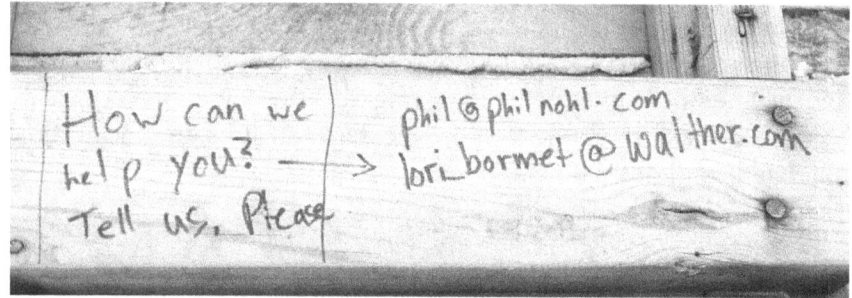

Message above the arch between the dining and living rooms

Originally, he had come to Joplin to help others in need, but as he stood there in humility, acknowledging God's hand in filling all the holes in his life, he realized that it was he who was the benefactor of God's blessings. All the effort he had put forth and the determination to serve his fellow man had filled his soul, changed his heart, and his eyes were opened to the blessings that had been brought into his and Lori's lives.

"I don't want to leave here," he said, placing the marker inside the broken coffee cup.

"What do you mean?" she asked.

"I feel welcome here, like this is where we belong. Home doesn't feel like home right now... this feels like home."

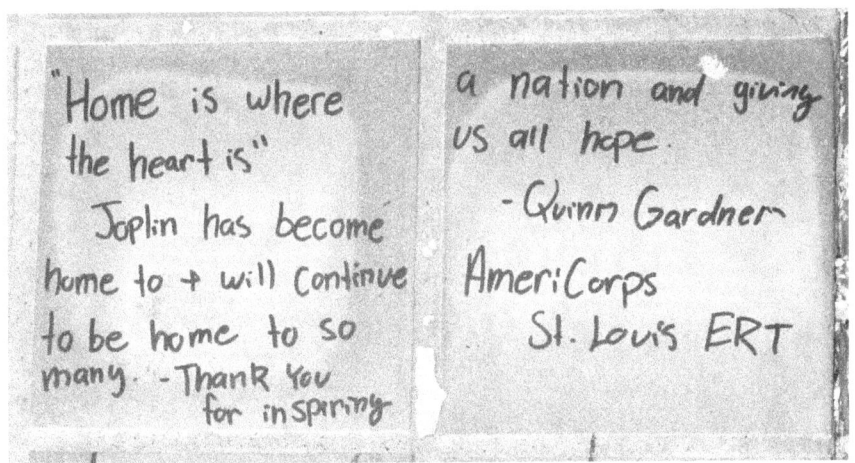

Message on fireplace floor tiles

"Then why don't we stay another week?"

"I was hoping you would say that. I know there's still more we need to do here and it feels good to be an instrument in God's hands, serving these people who desperately need help."

Phil walked over to Lori and pulled her close to him with his arm around her shoulder, expressing his love and appreciation for her. He realized that he had been holding her at arm's length from his heart. The pain of a previous relationship had subconsciously prevented him from letting her get close to his heart.

Life is too short, he thought, *to waste it on negativity or to live in the past. There is no guarantee of even one more day, so we make the best of each day and every moment we have. Rather than hoping things will be different or waiting for them to get better, we need to make things better in our lives... today.*

With a new sense of appreciation for life, happiness, love, hope, and joy, Phil and Lori walked hand in hand to their car, returning to the church for another week of service.

Messages on wall studs in the hallway

During the coming weeks and months, I continued to return to the house for various reasons. Each time I would return there were dozens and dozens more messages and signatures left on the house. All the walls that remained standing had been completely covered and now the messages were appearing everywhere else.

They were on the wall studs, door jambs, in the closets, on the doors, on the marble floors, on the window sills, on the bricks, on

182

Messages on a home school desk

the floor tiles, on the fireplace floor tiles, on the wood floors, on the coffee table, on the dining room table, on the glass of the china hutch, inside the closets, inside the pantry, on the outside of the house, on the light switch plates, on plumbing pipes, on the desk, and on the toys. There were even messages written on the magic broom. And then they started signing t-shirts and even a sports towel which they nailed to the outside of the south wall.

T-shirts and a sports towel signed and nailed to outside wall

During one of my visits back to the house, I found a note with a brick placed on top of it, sitting on the back steps. It was a note from the city, telling the residents that there was a deadline approaching in which any remaining debris had to be cleaned off the property, or an intent to rebuild had to be filed with the city.

I knew at that moment that there was no way I could either rebuild over or tear down what was, in my opinion, a giant *Get Well Soon Card* from the volunteers to the people of Joplin. I remembered my previous conversation with Patrick, and what he had said about the city wanting to preserve the south wall.

The south wall may be cool, I thought, *but the inside of the house is awesome. There's no way they could take part of it without taking it all*!

When I got home, I sent an email to Patrick. *I know you want to save the south wall*, I wrote, *but if you haven't been on the inside lately, you need to see what's written there, by the volunteers.*

I received an email a few days later, telling me that the city was interested in saving the entire setting as a historical artifact.

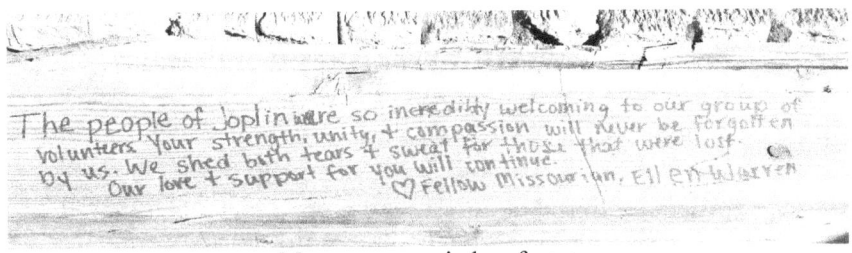

Message on a window frame

I was pretty excited to read that email. I knew the events of the tornado were only going to happen once in all our lifetimes – those who lived through it and those who came to our rescue. It is important to preserve the history of the event, but even more so, when the real story is the *intangible* human spirit.

The next morning, Jason and his crew had just pulled into town, stopping for coffee at the local mall. They were met there by a cheery, smiling, young barista who dutifully provided them with refreshments. They made small talk with some of the locals who gave them tips of sights to see while they were in town.

If they hadn't known any better, they would have had no idea that the pleasant town and its even more pleasant inhabitants had lived through such overwhelming destruction. But they did know better, because they had been watching the around-the-clock reports back home and following the story with a compassionate eye. In fact, it was the resoluteness and positivity of the people of Joplin that had inspired their road trip in the first place.

They had only been in Joplin a few minutes, but already courage and hopefulness was surprisingly abundant. As they made their way through town, Jason picked up a tablet that was sitting next to him on the seat and began jotting down some notes;

> *We have discovered people at every turn who had a good word to say or a helpful hand to lend. Encouraging messages were left on buildings and signs as temporary reminders to hold on, keep the faith and stay hopeful. One of the most memorable is one of the countless homes hit hardest by the storm. The house itself was stripped to its foundation, less two walls left standing. Scrawled across the top of one wall, in giant letters, "DOWN, <u>NOT OUT</u>!!"*

I had returned earlier that morning to do some cleaning in the basement, along with Abby and another of my granddaughters, Jacynda. We stopped to take a break under the deck in the back. While we were sitting in the shade, a man approached us, walking from the front of the house.

"Hello," he said, "we're looking for someone who might have signed the wall on the front of this house, or might know something about it."

Woman leaves message of Hope and Love from Cedar Rapids - Photo used with permission: © 2011 by Justin Hines / justinhines.com, All Rights Reserved

186

"This is our house," Abby said as we both stood up to greet him.

"That's awesome. We're shooting footage for a music video. Is there any way you could talk to us for a few minutes?"

"Yeah, we could probably do that," I said, following him to the front of the house.

At the front of the house was another man who was looking around the debris free rooms. He introduced himself as Jason, the director of the project, and gave me a brief overview of the message they were hoping to convey through their music video.

"We're shooting some footage for a new, Justin Hines music video. It will be used with one of his latest songs, 'Tell Me I'm Wrong,' which will be released soon."

My granddaughter, Jacynda, as she appears in the video - Photo used with permission: © 2011 by Justin Hines / justinhines.com, All Rights Reserved

He went on to explain that the inspirational messages spray painted on the house, resonated with Justin's outlook on life. Justin is a singer / song writer who has lived with physical impairments all his life. Triumph over adversity and the power of the human spirit are a driving force in his music and charitable causes.

"The theme of the video is going to be one of inspiration and hope. We'd like to shoot some footage of your family and your house to include in the video," he said, "is that something you'd be willing to do?"

"Yeah, that won't be a problem, as long as I don't have to dance."

As the camera man was setting up to shoot, Jason and I carried on a casual conversation.

"Why don't you want to dance?"

"Because I can't," I said, showing him my pathetic dance moves, which looked more like a human wind chime flapping around in the breeze.

"That's pretty good," he said, chuckling, "can you clap your hands over your head in rhythm?"

"Yeah, for one beat," I said, slapping my gloved hands together over my head.

For the next twenty minutes they shot film of us around the house. When they were getting ready to leave, a woman walked over from a car parked across the street. She had come from Iowa to help out. The crew filmed her writing a message, "Sending Hope and Love From Cedar Rapids" on the green wall.

Jason and his crew packed up their camera equipment and loaded it into their van. They thanked us for participating in the video and wished us the best of luck. Moments later, they drove out of sight.

Driving to their next location, Jason grabbed his tablet off the seat and continued writing where he had left off;
    It is a sentiment that seems to have a duplicitous purpose –

188

meant both as an offering of support to those in similar situations, and a rebellious battle cry in defiance to the storm itself.

As if to prove that sentiment was more than just words, the owner, Tim, dug his sofa, love seat, and coffee table out of the rubble and returned it to its rightful place in what once was his living room. This symbolic gesture offered a visual reminder to all that even in a place so stricken with grief, and even in a time where basic human necessities are so suddenly depleted, that rebuilding starts in the heart, that rebuilding has indeed begun, and the human spirit soars.

Jason then scribbled some production notes before tossing his tablet on the seat beside him.

Justin Hines, singer / song writer - Photo used with permission:

I had never heard of Justin before meeting his crew, but have become a big fan since then. The song and video were released a couple of months later and are very inspirational and uplifting. For me, it takes the listener / viewer through tragedy and the joy of overcoming obstacles and trials... finding your way home.

Tell Me I'm Wrong

If I ever lose my sense of pride
Turn my back on all I've known
If I ever feel like I've fallen behind
Show me just how far I've grown

In this lonely state of mind
I can only walk alone
Ever searching just to find
My way home...my way home

Tell me I've fallen
Tell me I'm done
Tell me I'm wrapped inside your love
Tell me I'm bleeding
Tell me I'm lost
Or tell me I'm wrong

If I ever lose my place in time
I can't say I never will
For I may never fall in a line
Darlin', can you love me still?

'Cause in this lonely state of mind
I have only walked alone
Ever searching just to find
My way home...my way home

Tell me I've fallen
Tell me I'm done
Tell me I'm wrapped inside your love
Tell me I'm bleeding
Tell me I'm lost
Or tell me I'm wrong

During the first couple of months after the storm, there were many music videos produced both professionally and by amateurs alike that included our house. One theme that emerged from these independent videos had to do with *going home* or metaphorically, recovering from tragedy and going back to a previous state of life.

We were filmed, photographed, and interviewed by numerous newspapers, television stations, and documentary film crews. At one point, you couldn't watch the nightly news without seeing our house in the opening video montage of the newscast.

When camera crews come to town to do a story, whether it was the high school starting a new year (USA Today) or the high school football team preparing for the new season (ESPN), our house was always included in the footage used to visually depict the triumph of the human spirit over extreme conflict.

Me, giving an interview

Shortly after the tornado, a local TV reporter stopped by with his cameraman. He wanted to know if he could interview me and I agreed. As the cameraman began setting up his equipment, the reporter and I had a couple of minutes to visit off camera.

"I lived far enough away from the path of the tornado," he said, "that my house didn't suffer any damage. The next morning when I got up and drove around the affected neighborhoods and witnessed the damage and destruction I became sad and depressed. No matter how hard I tried to get over it I couldn't get past the sadness. It wasn't until I drove by your house and read the messages on your walls, that my spirits lifted. I knew at that moment that everything was going to be okay and that as a community we would get past this."

We were always willing to visit with the press and help in any way. We felt that the story needed to be told and it gave us the opportunity to thank the volunteers who came and the rest of the world for all they had done for our community. Even if it was just thinking about us or praying for us, it blessed our lives.

In the final episode of ABC's "Extreme Makeover Home Edition," our house was included three times and again in the cast's farewell video. It shows the cast and crew signing their names on the walls and studs of our house. The crew even built wooden walls and benches in Cunningham Park that people could sign, symbolic of the walls, stud frames, and furniture in our house.

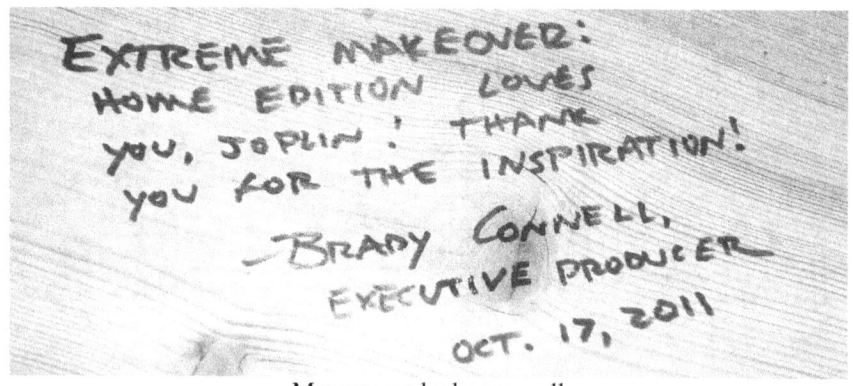

Message on bedroom wall

As time passed and the volunteers continued leaving more messages to the community, the significance of the house as an icon of the human spirit increased exponentially with each and every heartfelt message that was written. It soon became a shrine for the volunteers who referred to it as "the volunteer house" and "the signature house."

I've been asked many times, "why your house?" I believe that it simply had to do with how people connected at some spiritual or emotional level with one or more of the messages. There were more people than I can count who came by to tell me how much the messages on the walls had helped them cope with the tragedy. After giving a lot of thought to this question, there's no doubt in my mind that it comes down to four basic messages.

Message on wall stud

The first is faith. The first message I wrote was, "GOD BLESS JOPLIN!" That message appealed to a great many people. Many of the volunteers who poured into the streets were on a mission from God to provide for His *children*. Countless messages were penned with a spiritual theme and they often referenced scriptural passages. Joplin had experienced a real miracle, complete with angelic beings, along with divine intervention and protection.

The second is hope. As one blogger put it, referencing our house, "'DOWN, <u>NOT OUT</u>!!' is arguably the credo of the Joplin recovery efforts." Not only was it a message of hope to others, but it conveyed a tougher, more gritty message.

Message on pantry shelf

Like a champion boxer who dropped his guard for a second and took a sucker punch that temporarily rung his bell. All champions know the fight is not over because you get knocked down. As long as you keep getting up, the fight continues. The first punch never determines the outcome of the fight. The house stood tall amidst a landscape that in every direction was leveled to the ground, whether by the tornado itself or the machinery of the cleanup crews. It remained standing, as a beacon of hope.

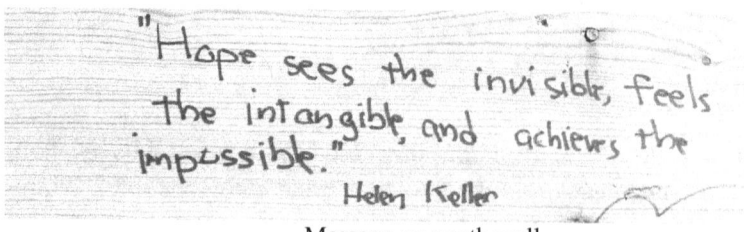

Message on south wall

The third is love. I believe this struck at the very heart of the volunteer and relief effort. Everyone who volunteered whether locally or from afar, wanted to make a difference in the lives of others who were in less fortunate circumstances.

The wall sized message of, "Thank You Volunteers - We ♥ U! - YOU ARE OUR HEROES!" let each of them know of our love and appreciation... that they were the real heroes. I read many posts and message boards where the volunteers mentioned that message on the wall and how much they appreciated it.

The fourth is the indomitable spirit of humankind. The phrase, "PRESS ON!" reminds us all that in spite of trials and difficulty we must still move forward, never surrendering. "It helps, I think, to consider ourselves on a very long journey: the main thing is to keep to the faith, to endure, to help each other when we stumble or tire, to weep and press on." - Mary Richards (main character of the Mary Tyler Moore show).

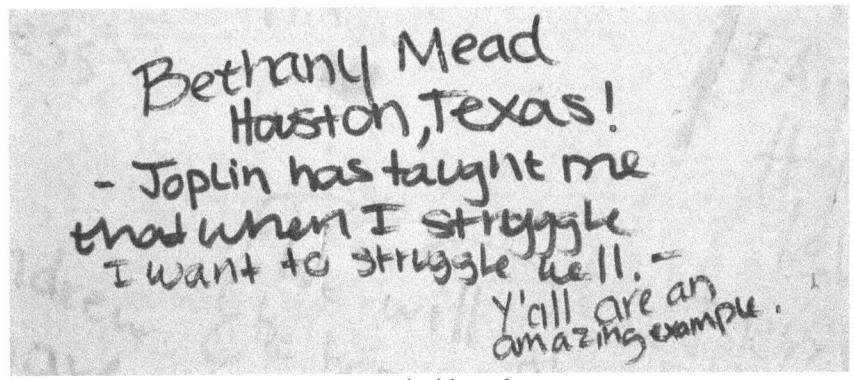

Message inside a closet

It's been said that, "nothing is more powerful than a message whose time has come." My original messages were just a small fire of hope burning in the cold darkness. Each person who signed their name or left a message to the community added another log to the fire, until the fire of hope burned warmly and brightly. All those messages came at a time when it was needed most.

Signatures on studs and wall
(more color photos, stories & information available at www.jthoh.com)

196

Chapter 9

In the ensuing weeks after the tornado, Stacey's ankle healed up...
not perfectly, but better. Her brother, Tim, also healed up and his
limp went away. Abby gave birth to a beautiful baby girl, Sophia.
The robins hatched their eggs and eventually left the nest. The
pilgrims sold their lot and a new house has been built there.

Even though I never found the USB drive that I was looking for, I
was able to retrieve the hard drive from my computer and extract
the data from it. After doing so, we were able to finish Stacey's
book ("Leadership Secrets For Healthcare") and get it published.

We moved from Joplin to the neighboring community of Carthage.
If you've ever seen the Andy Griffith show with Andy, Opie,
Barney, Gomer and Aunt Bea, then you get an idea of what
Carthage is like. Joplin is comparable to the neighboring
community of Mount Pilot in the show. It's the bigger town that
has two bowling alleys and stores that stay open all night long.

Originally, we had planned to rebuild in Joplin, but something
happened following the storm that I hadn't anticipated. Most of
our family members, including Max & Jaxon, began to show
symptoms of Post Traumatic Stress Disorder (PTSD).

It may be difficult to relate to it if you've never experienced it.
Even after many months, it's still a constant condition in our lives.
If the wind begins to blow hard, or there's a storm, or rain,
especially if there's any kind of tornado watch or warning, a wave
of panic goes over the entire family.

Our daughters have become amateur meteorologists as a result of
their PTSD. They are constantly monitoring the weather and
reviewing radar maps and forecasts. Perhaps that's a good thing
and will help them to be better prepared if another tornado ever
comes our way.

In many ways, things have returned back to normal, or at least as close as they can get. I still miss my garden, fruit trees, berry bushes and plants, but in time, I'll plant more. By the time I get that accomplished, I'll have more grandchildren who can help me.

Abby and Heather return to Joplin on a fairly regular basis to visit with friends or shop at the mall. On one of those trips in November, Abby was driving by the house to visit one of her friends. She noticed a group of people gathered in the yard and around the house. She stopped to see what they were doing.

There she met a group of artists who were capturing their feelings and impressions of the house in various mediums including oil, pastel, watercolor, marker, and pencil. It turns out they were a group of "Plein Air" artists. Plein Air is a french expression which means "in the open air."

Front of the house (dining room), done in pencil
Photo used with permission: © 2011 by Jesse McCormick, All Rights Reserved

A friend of the group, Linda, had taken a great interest in the house and convinced them to paint what she felt was a piece of history.

When the group arrived, all they really saw was a splintered wreck of a house sitting in the barren landscape of one empty and deserted lot after another. The whole area in the surrounding neighborhood was void of any color, absent any trees or foliage, with colorless, wind blown dirt everywhere they looked.

The artists were accustomed to painting in beautiful gardens and on streets lined with historic homes. The tattered house that had been suggested as subject matter was neither beautiful nor appealing to their artistic eyes.

Margie stood in the street, hesitant to proceed further, trying to convince herself that there was a reason to remove the art supplies from the back of her SUV. As she wrestled with the decision, she thought about the few months that had passed since the tornado. Like most of the other residents in town, she was still in blind shock and muddling through the devastation one day at a time. *If it hadn't been for the countless volunteers who had come to our aid,* she assured herself, *we would not have survived so well.*

Pondering these events, she came to realize that her soul and those of the community were being healed by the endless acts of human kindness. *We received HOPE,* she reminded herself, *from all over the world! The least I can do is take a look around and maybe get a glimpse of what Linda sees here.*

It was a bittersweet experience for her, walking around the splintered, tornado ravaged facade. She still felt empty and uninspired. *What does she possibly see in all this tornado debris?* she wondered as she approached the front of the house.

Respectful of her friend's request, she went forward, walking through the nonexistent entrance with her camera in tow. Immediately, she was drawn in by the messages written on the painted walls and the scriptures scratched on exposed lath boards. She was intrigued with the simple drawings of hearts and crosses.

She began reading the love notes that were so carefully worded to help others understand the heart and soul of the human spirit... and the HOPE left behind on the walls of this house.

It was not simply another shell of a house ravaged by the tornado as it appeared to be only minutes before. *This is a refuge to the weary volunteers*, she thought, *an inspiration to the people we now call friends, who toiled along side us, cried with us, who left with their lives and ours forever changed.*

Front of the house, done in oil

As she continued through the house, she began to see what Linda had seen and why she suggested they paint there. *This house*, she thought, *had become a symbol of HOPE and we became a people of HOPE... and that is a powerful God-breathed thing*!

Inspiration bubbled up from deep within, coursing through her and she enthusiastically started snapping pictures. Before long, she returned to the SUV for her supplies and upon setting up, began squeezing oil colors onto her palette.

Margie's style of painting was typically one of purpose and definition, with patient and deliberate discipline to detail, form, and composition. However, as she loaded her brush with vibrant colors, pressing it to the canvas, she was moved with unbridled passion and fury. Her hand may have held the brush, but it was her heart and soul that moved it so spiritedly across the canvas.

The results were unlike anything she had created before... energetic and emotionally charged bold strokes of wild colors... but in it all was HOPE, spray painted on the bare boards of the house in which the family had survived... that the artists now claimed as their own.

When Abby arrived at the house with Sophia, the artists took a break from their work so they could visit with her. They were interested in her story of riding out the storm in the basement, asking lots of questions. She told them about her experience and how things were, in general, since then.

Darlene, one of the painters who was working in watercolor, saw it as a symbol of hope to see Abby with Sophia, who had just recently come into the world after surviving in her mother's womb. *What a perfect metaphor*, she thought, *of the human spirit in going from tragedy to rebirth and renewal, to a restoration of hope*.

After Abby drove away Darlene returned to her painting. She guided her brush gently and slowly, masterfully transforming globs of colors into a work of art. She reflected upon the activities around town over the past several months. *Hundreds of thousands of people had come from all walks of life,* she thought, *from all over the country to provide assistance and relief.*

Thousands of these volunteers left a message or just signed their names as a reminder of their love and support. They have left a part of themselves behind, that has become a part of history and a critical part of the story that will be told for generations to come.

She stepped back from her easel, content with the artistic expression she had captured. She applied a few additional strokes of color before she was finished.

Front of the house, done in watercolor

This house, she mused, is like a blank canvas inviting the creative impetus. And from the many volunteer artists with sharpies in hand, a masterpiece of love is created. An artistic reminder indelibly etched into the heart and mind, of a horrific event that brought out the best of the human spirit.

Darlene wrote a poem about the butterfly people, that coincides with a painting she did for a local art exhibit that focused on identifying the positive aspects of the tragedy.

Butterfly People

Listen my children and you will hear
Of the tornado touching Joplin so near
Coming out from the darkness striking fear
Wrenching our hearts as we lost friends so dear

It was May 22 of eleven the year
The sirens were wailing sounding so sheer
Wind whipping houses and cars out of gear
Buildings and bricks flying they veer

Grinding up grit embedding eye and ear
But children saw the light perfectly clear
"Butterfly People" there to wipe the tear
Stop in the path and from danger steer

Story of a girl of three that night
Her mother shielding with all her might
Protecting her daughter as a car rolled right
Beside her as they huddled in fright

When telling the tale of her tornado plight
Mother recounted the car did alight
By her shoulder stopped and touched them tight
But the daughter challenged her mother quite

By saying "no mommy" not to be trite
The car did not stop by itself from its flight
But the Butterfly People protected from sight
Stood in the path so the pair was alright

"Butterfly People," done in watercolor

When Abby arrived at her friend's house, she called me on the phone.

"Hey dad," she said, "you'll never guess who's at our house."

"Who?"

"A group of artists are painting pictures of the house. I stopped to talk to them for a few minutes. I told them we were there when the tornado went through."

"Where are you now?"

"At Maddison's house."

"Drive back over there and see if you can get some names and contact information so I can get ahold of them. I'd like to see the paintings they're working on. Sprint over there now and see if you can get them to write down their email addresses and phone numbers."

Over the next couple of days, I contacted each of the artists who were there. I wanted to know if I could get a picture of their finished artwork. They all sent me pictures of what they had done. It was amazing to see the difference in each artist's impression and how they captured the house.

One of the artists, Crystal, had captured the house from the back, where "PRESS ON!" was spray painted on the arch above where the stove had been. She told me that there was some red paint exposed in the pantry area. In her interpretation she saw it as a red heart (appearing in the very center of the artwork) to symbolize the love for our family and the people of Joplin.

Back of the house, done in pastels

To me, that is one of the most amazing things about original works of art. Something like the paint flaking away and exposing some red paint beneath it is transformed into a wonderful symbol of love. I am so very appreciative of that symbolism because that's what the entire house represents.

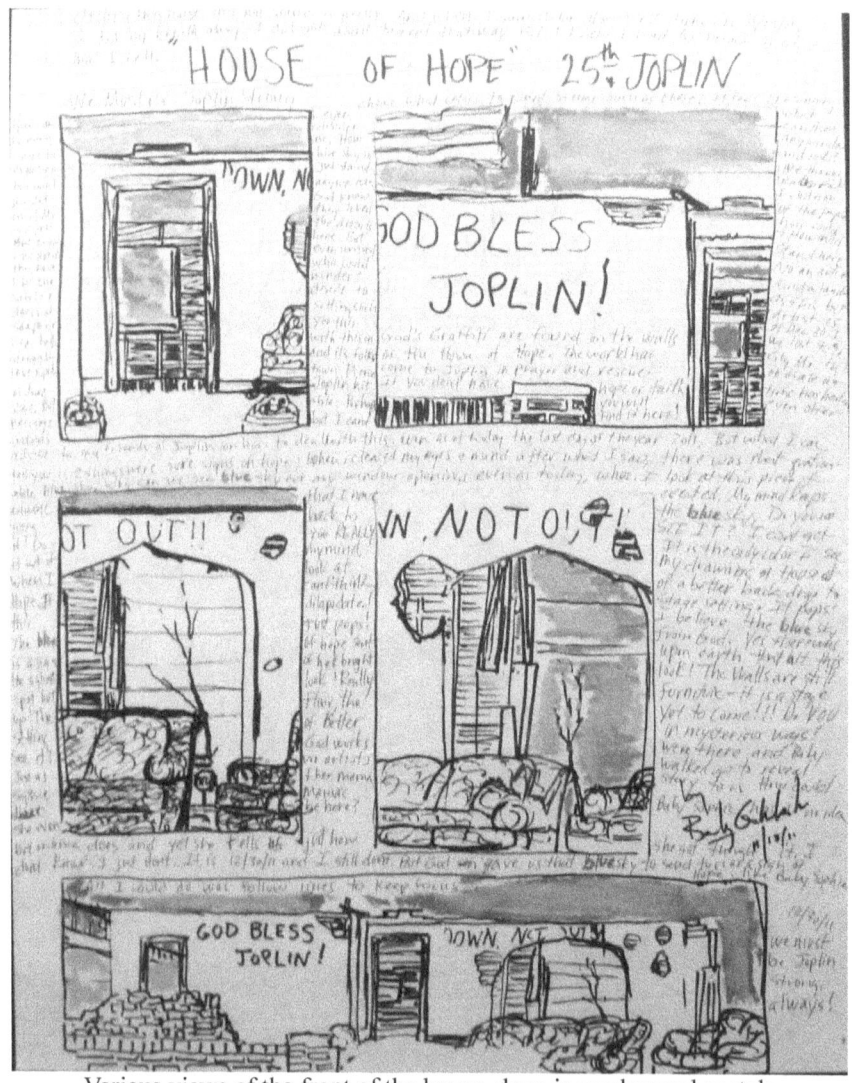

Various views of the front of the house, done in marker and pastels

She told me she wanted to give me the artwork that she had done. I didn't know what to say. I basically have no artistic talent (in addition to not being able to dance), so I'm in awe of those who do. I was thrilled at the thought that she would want me to have her original work of art.

"I would love to have it," I told her, "but you don't have to give it to me. I would be happy with just a picture of it."

"I knew when I started on it," she insisted, "that I wanted to give it to you when it was finished."

Not only did she give me the picture, already beautifully framed, but she brought me a "Precious Moments" ceramic figurine of a child holding a heart that said, "Love Is The Best Gift Of All."

How wonderful is that, I thought, *and how often does that ever happen in your lifetime?* My life has been touched in so many ways, by so many wonderful people and I'm constantly amazed by their love and generosity.

I continued to go back to the house every week or so, to take pictures of the new signatures and messages left by the volunteers who continue to come to Joplin. Quite often I would meet different groups who had come by to see the house. Usually, when they learned that my family and I were there through the tornado they wanted to hear our story and ask questions.

Many people who, after hearing our story, told me that I needed to write a book about our experience and how the House of Hope came to be. I was reassured by many that our story was one that needs to be told, because it will forever remember and honor the many volunteers and their contributions.

The more I considered it the more I knew that I did need to write a book. Rather than dwell on the negative aspects of the tornado or even the statistics, I wanted to celebrate all the goodwill and the overwhelming spiritual energy that has forever changed so many lives for the better in our area, around the country, and even around the world.

A Christmas tree that someone had decorated and placed in the living room

By the time Thanksgiving came and went I decided to begin writing. It was an emotional process, going back and reliving the events of that time. Fortunately, there are many more positive things that have come from our experiences. And more good continued as I met wonderful people at the house, all the time.

In early December I went to take some pictures of the new messages that had been written since my last visit. Much to my surprise, one of Santa's helpers had set up a Christmas tree in the living room. It was a live evergreen tree set up in a stand with several colored glass ornaments hanging on it.

The star that adorned the top of the tree was one that had been made by some member of the community months earlier. The city had an event where people could come together and paint blank, hand cut wooden stars in whatever way they were inspired. The stars were then attached to wooden stakes and pounded into the ground in the areas around town that were hardest hit.

Whoever put up the tree must have felt inspired to use one of those stars for the House of Hope Christmas tree. The star they selected was painted red with yellow trim around the edge. There were words in green paint; "Faith, Hope, Love, Today, Tomorrow, Forever" hand painted on the points of the star and in the center.

It couldn't have been a more perfect addition to the house. The symbolism of the Christmas tree and the star that was selected to top it off really resonated with what the house had become and will forever be.

Shortly before Christmas I got a call from Arthur, a reporter with the New York Times. He told me he was doing a story on the continued progress of the cleanup and the volunteers who kept coming to Joplin. The story was going to include information about the monument that had been erected in Cunningham Park. The park was located across the street from St. John's hospital and had taken a direct hit from the tornado.

Monument erected in Cunningham Park as a tribute to the volunteers

Apparently, when he was gathering information from various volunteer groups and people associated with the volunteer efforts, he kept being told that he needed to see "the volunteer house." He came to Joplin and went to the house to take a look for himself.

I asked if he'd seen anything like it before and like all the others I had asked in the past, he confirmed that not only was it amazing, but he had never seen anything quite like it before. He also observed the stark contrast of the warm, organic shrine the house had become, to the cold concrete and metal tribute in the park.

A few days later, on Christmas eve, many miles away at a church in Illinois, Phil stepped forward to a wooden pulpit. He was facing a crowd of worshippers who had gathered together to celebrate the birth of the Savior. He pulled a piece of paper from his shirt pocket upon which he had written his sermon for the congregation. Many emotions began to fill his heart and soul as he contemplated the message he was about to deliver.

He started by telling a story that had begun several months before, of a man who lived in Texas. This man heard the calling of God and when he answered, he left behind his home and his job. The call would take him almost five hundred miles away to a place he had never before seen.

This man's name was Howard. He was a skilled carpenter and knew that God needed his skills to help in the rebuilding efforts in Joplin. Three days after the devastating tornado, Howard had arrived to help. He didn't know beforehand where he would be needed, but trusted in God to give him direction.

He very quickly made a connection with a local church and began to minister to those affected by the tornado, by building wooden sheds. There was a great need for sheds to help people store their belongings that had been strewn throughout their neighborhoods. In addition to building sheds he also assisted families who had no insurance, in rebuilding their homes and ultimately, their lives.

As Phil continued with his message, he likened Howard to the humble David who slew Goliath.

"David defeated Goliath," he said, "not because of skill or luck, but because he had the knowledge that the armies of God were behind him. The armies of God are behind Howard."

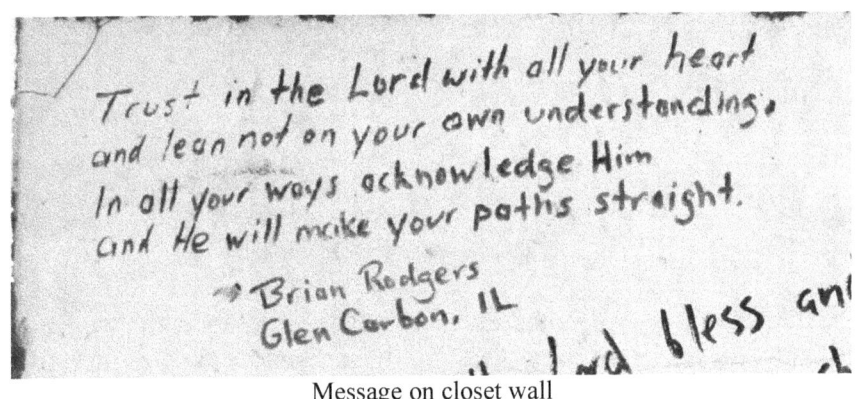

Message on closet wall

Before he and Lori had returned to Aurora, Howard told him that he planned on staying in Joplin for another year or longer, just to help others with rebuilding.

"Since going to Joplin, there is one theme," Phil continued, "one life promise that seems to have been driven home time and time again. God will take care of us when we need it, and His plan is bigger than anything you can ever imagine or even will into being."

Phil then recounted the many little miracles that happened throughout his stay in Joplin, of meeting Howard and learning the carpentry skills that he would need later. How his confidence had grown and his understanding of life, and relationships, and the importance of never taking one moment for granted.

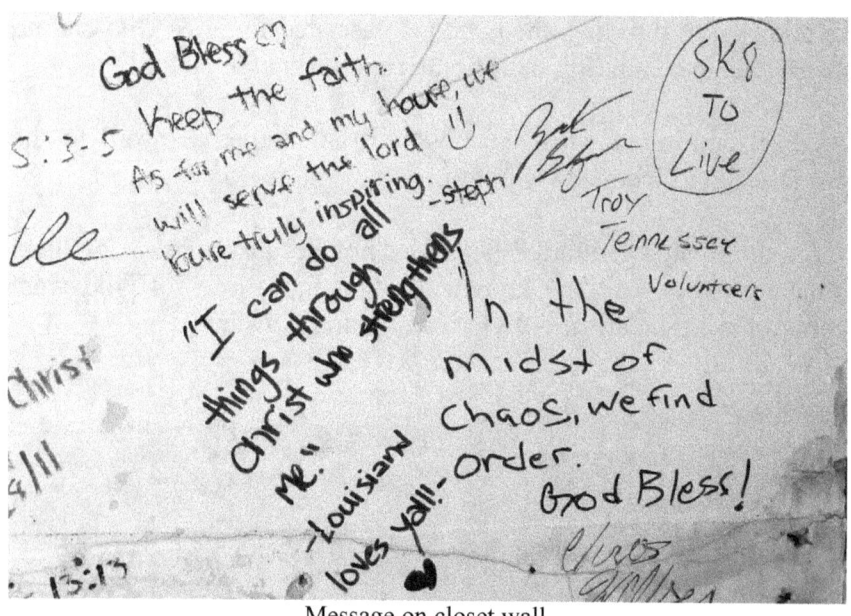

Message on closet wall

"I stand before you today, and I'm not anyone special," he said, looking at Lori's smiling face in the audience, "I am just any ordinary person. I was wandering around without any real direction, just trying to make sense of my life. And then I heard God's call to Joplin."

He felt a lump welling up in his throat that caused him to pause momentarily. He could feel his lower lip begin to tremble as he forced the words out of his mouth.

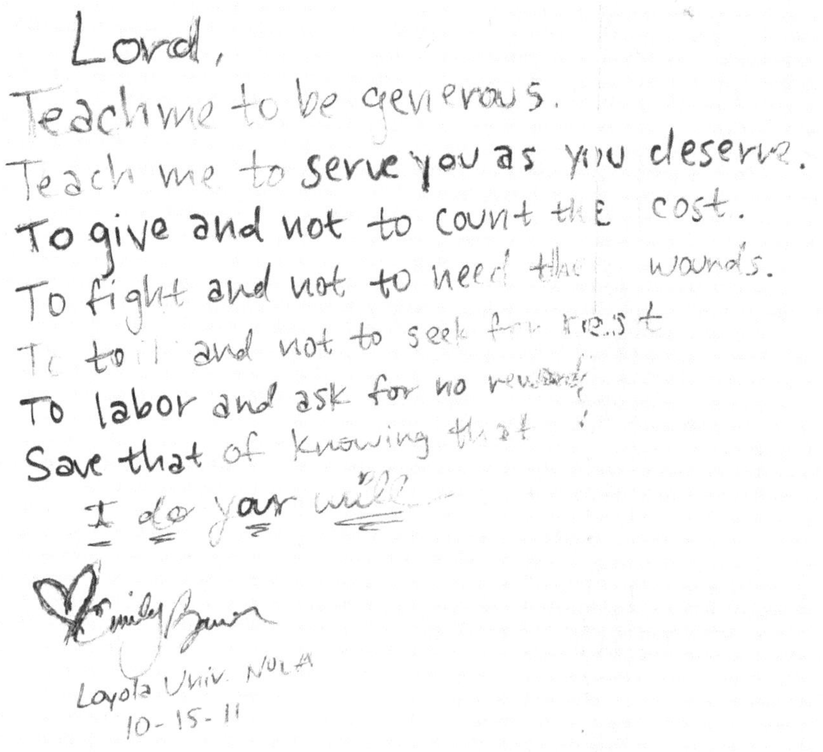

Lord,
Teach me to be generous.
Teach me to serve you as you deserve.
To give and not to count the cost.
To fight and not to heed the wounds.
To toil and not to seek for rest
To labor and ask for no reward
Save that of knowing that
I do your will.

Emily Brun

Loyola Univ. NOLA
10-15-11

Message on stairwell door

"God took me and spun me around and worked through me in helping countless numbers of people. And in the end, I look back and realize that I got more out of it than I could have ever imagined. I did one thing and through the work of God, I was helped tenfold... and I never saw it coming. Neither did Howard... neither did David... neither did Joseph and Mary. When they were called, they answered and did the Lord's bidding."

As Phil raised his eyes, observing the congregation, he could see that his message was being received by the hearts of the listeners. Many tears were being wiped away as he spoke the words he knew

God wanted them to hear.

"I pray that God will help us listen, to just stop and listen to the Master's voice and be ready when He calls. We need to let go of our own wants and find out what God wants for us. *For whosoever will save his life, shall lose it: and whosoever will lose his life for my sake, shall find it.* Put your trust in God, answer the call, lose your life and you will find it, and like mine and all the others who answered His call, your life will be infinitely better in ways you can't even imagine!"

Phil paused and finding Lori in the crowd, gazed adoringly into her eyes, knowing that her life had been changed for the better, just as his had. Their experience in answering God's call had forged a bond between them that brought them to a higher level of spirituality, unity, conviction, and mutual respect. They would forever be grateful for the mighty changes that God had wrought in their hearts as they lost their lives in serving the people of Joplin.

"Please join with me in singing 'Oh Holy Night' as we thank God for sending His Son to this earth, who came to save us all."

Message on bedroom wall

Message on dining room wall

Like so many volunteers who had come to serve, Phil and Lori's lives had been forever transformed by the Love of God, manifested through them as they ministered to those in need.

For our family, Christmas day was different this year than those of the past. It was a much more special time for us. Having gone through the tornado and been snatched from the jaws of death was especially significant. Rather than focusing on the gift giving and things that weren't really important, we focused on the true meaning of Christmas, in remembering the greatest gift of all... the birth of the Lamb of God, who died to save us all.

The day after Christmas, I was excited to see that the New York Times ran the story of the house in the paper and on their website. As a result, the story was picked up and run in nearly every online news website in the nation. It even generated interest outside the U.S. I was called and interviewed by the Canadian Broadcasting Corporation, the most listened to radio station in Canada.

The New York Times story was entitled, "For Joplin, a Love Letter in Ruins." In a very real and literal sense, our house is a love letter. It is written from the volunteers to the residents of Joplin and all those who have come to help. It was born from the ruins of the storm and continues to remind the community of the love and service given so freely, by so many.

The New York Times story ends by saying that, "...the house stands, oddly resilient to the deconstructive power of the storm and the constructive power of the rebuilding city, speaking to a moment in between that will be harder to explain when it's gone."

The house still standing in winter, topped with snow

Once the story ran and appeared everywhere in the press, I started getting calls from the local newspapers and television stations for interviews and plans for the house. I believe the New York Times story was a wake up call to rescue this treasure that was being damaged by the elements, and the urgency of getting it preserved.

My desire to have it preserved isn't so much that it was our house, as it could have been any other house. It's because of what it represents, not only to our family, but the rest of the community, the country and to some extent, the world. It is the heart, the voice and the soul of the people who poured into the streets to ease the pain and suffering of a ravaged community in the heart of America.

The house sat out in the elements for the better part of eight months. Much of the paint has flaked off the green and yellow walls, erasing the messages and signatures once there. The sun has faded and bleached many more. As more volunteers have come behind, they have left new messages, words of love, hope, and inspiration in their place, but many of the original messages are forever lost to the elements.

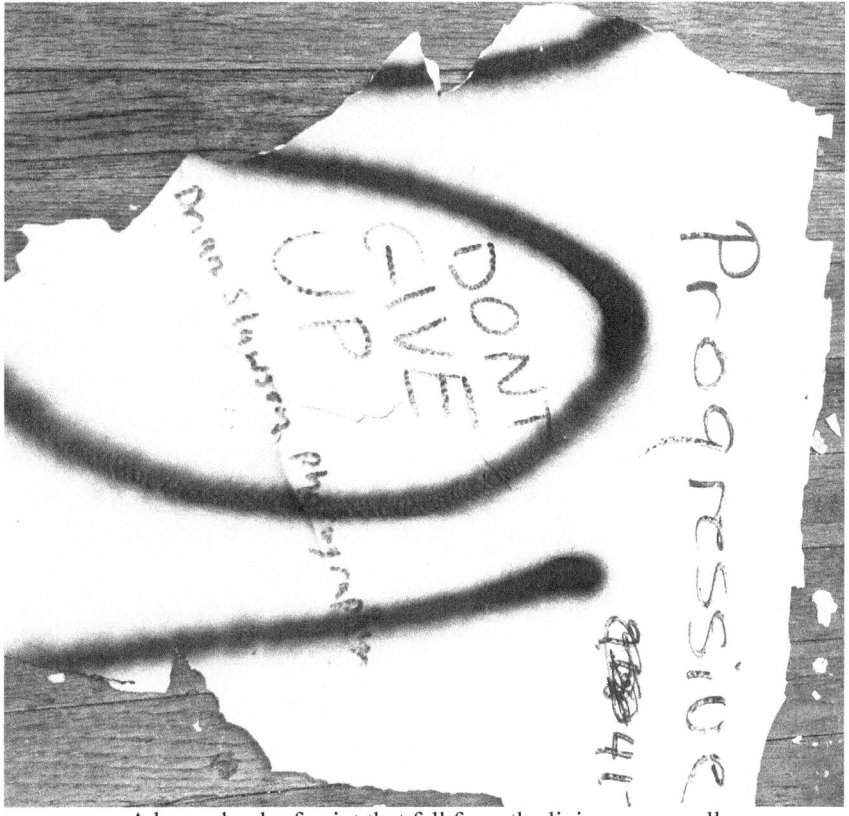
A large chunk of paint that fell from the living room wall

By early January, I was contacted by Patrick to let me know that there were some groups of people who wanted to join forces and shrink wrap the entire structure of the house above the foundation.

Saving bricks and construction work, preparing for shrink wrap

This would help keep the interior of the house out of the elements and prevent any further damage, until a museum could be built.

By late January, efforts to preserve the house were well under way. David, from Glenn Group Commercial Development was working with Steve and his crew from Willey Construction, to build wall frames and roof trusses to support the shrink wrap materials, allowing for moisture runoff. Jose and his crew from Tracker Marine would then install the shrink wrap materials to enclose and protect the house against further damage from the elements.

Chad was working with a crew from Americorps, who meticulously removed the brick from the house and porch. They chipped away the mortar from the bricks and stacked them on pallets. The bricks will be used later to restore the house to the condition it was in, before the preservation efforts began.

On January twenty-fourth, there was a press conference held at the front of the house. Patrick, David, Jose, Chad and I were there to answer any questions concerning the house and its preservation.

218

"We're here today," Patrick told the press, "to begin the process of preserving this house, that has become an oasis of hope. It has become a refuge for the volunteers who have come to Joplin to help us recover from the storm. Here, the volunteers could take a break and enjoy a cold drink. They left messages of faith, hope, love, and inspiration for the community. It is important to preserve this piece of history, because it will help us tell the story of the miracle of the human spirit that took place in our community."

He then went on to describe the details of how the construction crew built a framework around and over the house to support the shrink wrap materials. He described the shrink wrap process and how the house would be transported to a temporary location until it could be moved into the museum.

Preparing for the shrink wrap materials

"When we place this house in the museum," he continued, "we will rebuild the back deck and front porch, just as it was after the tornado, from the original lumber and bricks we saved. We will restore the bricks to the sides of the house, like they were a few days ago. All the furniture and other items that are here now, will stay here and be set up in the museum just as it is today."

"Tim," Patrick said jokingly, looking over his shoulder toward me, "you don't want to keep any of this furniture, do you?"

"Not at all," I said, smiling.

Shortly after the press conference ended, Jose and his crew attached the huge sheets of shrink wrap material to enclose the structure and sealed it snugly.

Signature on door jamb with a painting of an angel and a child

Once the museum is built, the plan is to place the house there, in its entirety. The deck on the back will be restored. The front porch will be rebuilt from the saved brick. The inside building materials of the house will be preserved, encased in some type of sealant. The furniture will remain inside, in its current condition. The house will be included in its entirety and people will be able to walk through it just like when it was on the original street lot.

By mid February, the house had been moved off the foundation, and transported to its new temporary home. Orren, of Tilton & Sons House Moving, removed it from the foundation, transporting it by truck to a temporary site. There it will sit in its protective cocoon until it is moved to its final resting place in the museum.

Message on stairwell door jamb

That's the good news. The bad news is that while these latest efforts will preserve what remains now, what has been lost due to the elements can never be reversed or replaced. Hence, the appropriately titled newspaper article about a love letter in ruins.

The main purpose of this book is to forever preserve and honor those wonderful volunteers and their invaluable contributions not only in rebuilding our town, but in rebuilding our hope and helping us to press on, when it would have been so easy to give up.

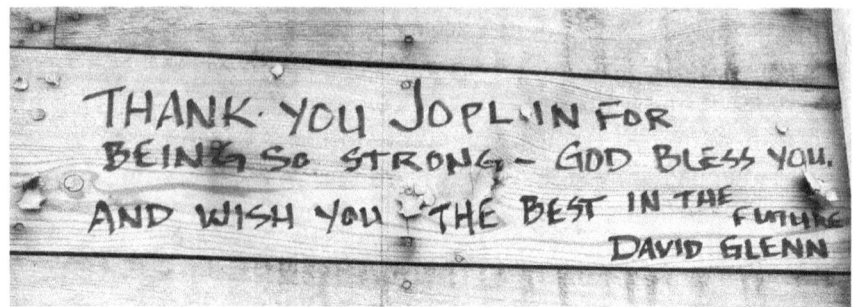

Messages on outer wall

Messages on wall stud and closet wall
(more color photos, stories & information available at www.jthoh.com)

222

Chapter 10

When I contacted the artists who had done paintings of our house, I received an unexpected email from Margie. She told me that she felt inspired to paint original artwork for the cover of my book if God willed it. She had never before met me, nor seen any content from my book. All she knew is that I was writing a book about the house as a tribute to the volunteers.

We had tentatively agreed to meet and discuss ideas for the cover. I totally dropped the ball and ended up thinking that she was working on ideas that we would discuss later. When it came time to start thinking about the cover, I realized much to my horror, that I had dropped the ball and may not have left her enough time to create anything inspirational, much less a masterpiece.

I was almost too embarrassed to contact her, but I did. I hoped she might forgive me and agree that a mind is indeed a terrible thing to waste. I was hopeful that maybe she was still interested and could meet the deadline.

Fortunately, she was and she did... and as you can see from the covers of this book, she did an amazing job. The cover artwork is an inspirational masterpiece that not only captures the essence of the House of Hope, but in many ways, the essence of the whole chain of events that began in May 2011 and continue on.

Painting and message / drawing on bedroom wall

When I was reviewing the finished cover artwork with her, it was suggested that maybe she and some of the other artists come over to the house on a Sunday afternoon and do some paintings inside, since the house was sealed from the elements.

I thought that would be a great idea and since there was no way for anyone to get in the house, it would be something special when the house is unwrapped at some future date.

Clown painted on wall stud

I arrived at the house a few minutes before Margie and Jesse showed up. While I was waiting, David came driving through the alley and stopped. He told me that the house movers were going to start preparing the house for moving the next day.

What are the chances of us getting into the house to add a splash of color at the last possible opportunity before the house is moved? I had no previous knowledge that the house movers would be starting on Monday. In fact, I was under the impression that it would be several more weeks before they started.

Later, when I had just finished writing this book and was preparing it for the publisher, I received another unexpected email from Margie. She told me about another artist she had met, with an inspirational story she thought might be worthy to add to the book. When I learned more about him and his story, I agreed.

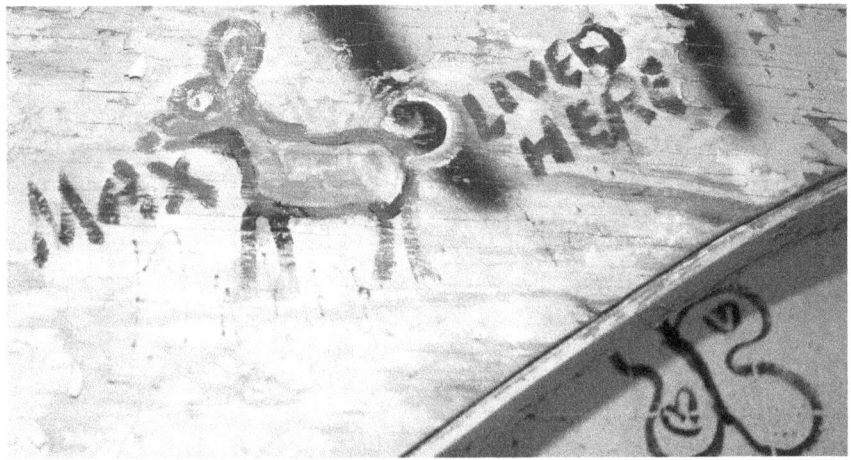
Painting of Max on kitchen arch and butterfly on the wall behind it

Even though this artist, Vincent, never painted any pictures of our house, his story and actions are another example of the healing powers of service, faith, hope, love, and inspiration. Not only that, but I'm a big fan of graffiti art and his is pretty cool stuff!

His story begins like many others. After hearing the tornado warnings, he immediately took shelter with his mother in the basement of her home in Carthage. While they waited for the storm to pass, he received a message telling him that a family member's home in Joplin had been hit by the tornado.

What about the children, he thought, fearing the worst for his niece and nephews. Without thought for their own safety, he and his mother left their shelter and drove directly toward the storm.

By the time they reached Joplin the tornado had disappeared silently into the sky. Unfortunately, it had left its mark on the landscape, carved through the very heart of Joplin. What he saw when they drove through the dark, unlit streets, and ravaged neighborhoods will be forever embedded into his memory.

Painting on building wall

The town his family had called home for years and to where he had recently moved, was in ruins. Upon reaching his family's home, he was overjoyed to find them unharmed, having survived in a closet. After helping others in the neighborhood, he returned to Carthage with his family, where they would be able to better care for the children and get them safely to bed.

The next morning, Vincent and his wife, Jessie, returned to Joplin to assist with the search and recovery efforts that were underway. During the next few days they transitioned into having more involvement in the cleanup efforts.

After a week and a half of volunteering, it was necessary for Vincent to return to his regular work. The efforts that he had tirelessly devoted to the community had taken a toll on him, depleting his spiritual, mental, and emotional reserves.

He wished there was more he could do to help ease the suffering of his community. He knew that his city needed to have their spirits lifted, to help them get through so great a tragedy.

During the coming days, he agonized over what he could do to make any significant difference in the lives of others. On the one hand, he and his family had been spared, and for that he was grateful. But on the other, so many others were not so fortunate and he felt an overwhelming need to provide some relief.

He awoke from a dream one morning with a vivid recollection of it still fresh in his mind. In his dream he was in his youth, a boy growing up in Buffalo, New York.

He saw himself walking down a quiet, empty street with a backpack slung over his shoulder. The bag made a clunking and clanking sound with every step he took. It was late and the streets were dark, with the exception of a full moon and the occasional street lights.

He stopped at a building alongside the street that was dark and deserted. There were no people visible on the street in either direction. Vincent removed the bag from his shoulder and lowered it gently to the ground. Reaching into the bag, he removed a can.

Painting on building wall

There was just enough light from the moon and a distant street light to see the wall clearly. He started shaking the can vigorously as he stepped closer to the colorless, light gray wall. He extended his arm and pressed the nozzle on the top of the can.

He guided his hand skillfully over the wall as paint hissed from the can with every stroke. He walked to the left and then to the right, applying bursts of color methodically to the wall.

228

When he was satisfied with what he had done, he returned to his bag for another can and continued to repeat the process of applying additional colors.

Once he was finished with his art mural, he quickly gathered the cans from the ground and stowed them in his backpack. He quickly walked away from what, in reality, was a crime scene.

Vincent laid in his bed, replaying the dream over and over in his mind. He wished that he could have been recognized for his artistic expressions when he was younger. Instead, graffiti at that time was not seen as an art form by those outside his circle. At that point in his life, his talent would have to remain in the shadows.

As he pondered upon his dream and the days of his youth, he reminded himself that art, in any medium, can lift and revitalize the human spirit, especially when it is fashioned to fill the void of emptiness and despair.

He arose from his bed with a passionate desire to return to the hardest hit areas of town, hoping to paint something inspirational. It didn't matter to him whether it was on a wrecked car, destroyed house, or abandoned building, he just wanted to create something colorful and inspirational to compete with the dull and depressed landscape that prevailed in that part of town.

He called Jim, a fellow artist he met at a graffiti art event the previous year. Jim agreed to meet him and locate some places where they could paint and hopefully, inspire others.

The first place they went was to the Salvation Army (across the street from our house), but were denied because the building was structurally unsound and needed to come down.

They found another location at the corner of Twentieth Street and Main Street. There, next to the gas station / convenience store was a bare brick wall painted with a neutral beige color.

Painting on building wall

The building was presently being occupied by a karate studio. The two men rushed inside and presented the owners of the studio with their idea to paint a mural on the outside wall. The owners were delighted with the idea and gave them permission to get started.

With no sketches or drawings to go by, the two artists began to paint whatever came to mind. Before long, the wall was covered with inspirational words and pictures they hoped would catch people's eyes and provide something of beauty amid the ugly destruction that surrounded them.

No sooner had they completed the mural than it began to garner the attention of the local residents who thanked them for their uplifting works of art. Many people signed their names on the wall and before long, the news media were contacting them for interviews.

The wall soon became known as "the Hope Wall."

Vincent had completed two other ("HOPE" and "RESTORE") individual paintings that he and the Extreme Makeover Home Edition crew auctioned off for a local charitable organization.

He continues to partner with other businesses and organizations in the community, providing additional works of art and murals. He hopes to beautify the city and restore the hopes and dreams of his friends and neighbors.

Picture of the "HOPE" painting
Photo used with permission: © 2011 by Vincent Alejandro, All Rights Reserved

One of the most powerful and destructive forces of nature crushed the city of Joplin. But from that, forces much greater than those of the destruction began to rise up and renew the city. Beauty emerged and began to flourish, fueled only by the human spirit.

231

I've heard it said that flowers must be crushed in order to release the perfume inside them. It is a very fitting metaphor of our fair community and those who came to our aid. Sometimes we need to be crushed in order to bring out the best of the human spirit that resides in each of us.

Painting on building wall
Photo used with permission: © 2011 by Vincent Alejandro, All Rights Reserved

The people I've met and the events that have happened which led me to write this book are too coherent and linear to be just dumb luck or coincidental. I can't help but believe that there was a guiding force directing my path to cross with the many wonderful people who exemplify so well, what I had hoped to capture and share in this book.

I am hopeful that it doesn't end there. I am optimistic that the outpouring of love can and will continue. I created a special website (www.jthoh.com) that links to a social network page. The website is also listed in the front pages of this book.

There you will find a place where anyone can post pictures and tell their own volunteer stories of serving or being served. A place where people can write their names on an electronic wall, rather than a wall that crumbles in the elements. A place where their comments will never fade. A place where pictures can be shared for all to see, a place where people can connect with others who touched their lives. A resource that will compliment the museum.

I hope that everyone who reads this book will tell others of this website so that everyone who was involved in the relief efforts can contribute to a one-of-a-kind tribute to the volunteers and the miracle of the human spirit.

I hope that those who were involved in any way will post pictures and write stories of their experiences to share with others. I hope to see an outpouring of love and inspiration from people all over the country and all over the world. How often do you ever get to be a part of something so wonderful and uplifting?!

It has been an amazing and faith promoting experience to witness the many miracles that have occurred throughout the tornado recovery efforts. There can never be enough thanks given to all the people, groups, and organizations who came to our rescue.

There were volunteers who represented every U.S. state, Puerto Rico, Costa Rica, Canada, Ireland, and other locations. They traveled over great distances and at great personal sacrifice and effort to help us cleanup and rebuild our city.

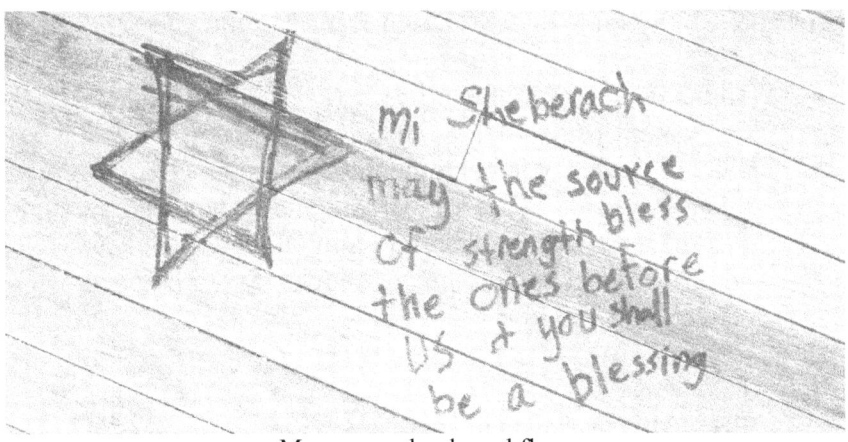
Message on hardwood floor

There were volunteers from virtually every religious affiliation who came to minister to us and serve the physical and spiritual needs of our community. They answered God's call to serve and helped heal our wounds, restore our hope, and strengthen our faith. They were like the Good Samaritan on steroids!

Painting and messages on closet wall

All of these efforts have been heralded as "the miracle of the human spirit" and I add my personal witness, testimony, and firsthand experience that what happened here truly is nothing short of a miracle... one that keeps repeating itself, over and over again.

I think the feelings of all those who provided assistance and came to our aid can be summed up through Jason's sentiments;

> To the people of Joplin:
> On behalf of Justin Hines and his entire team, we wish you the very best as you continue in your struggle to overcome this dark event. Please know that you are in our hearts, and that there are people like us all around the world, who admire your strength, who are in awe of your courage, who are sending you love.
>
> Jason Gileno
> Justin Hines Management Team
> Director of "Tell Me I'm Wrong" Music Video

234

"You are the light of the world. A city on a hill cannot be hidden." Stay strong Joplin. You are an inspiration to Christians everywhere. We LOVE you! God bless the USA.
— Rachel Zumbek 10/9/11

Message on hardwood floor

Sunshine and hope break through the dark clouds over the House of Hope

Jack's drawing on closet wall

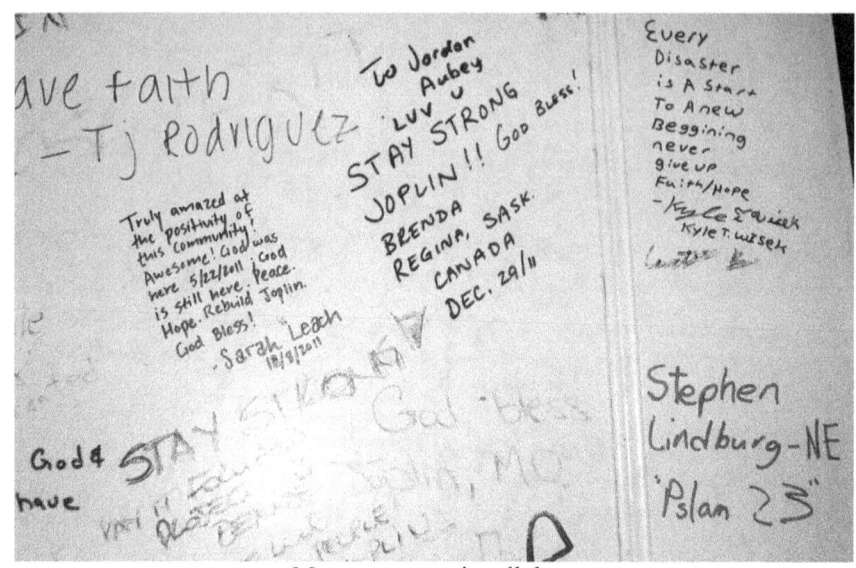

Messages on stairwell door

Message on bedroom wall

236

Message on pantry wall

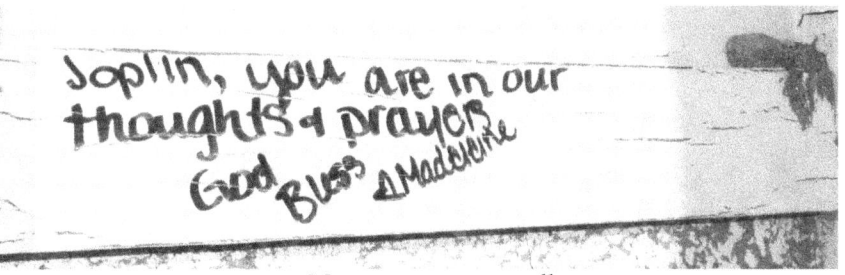

Message on pantry wall

GOD BLESS ALL THOSE FACING STRIFE & DESTRUCTION IN THEIR LIFE. EC

Message on door jamb

237

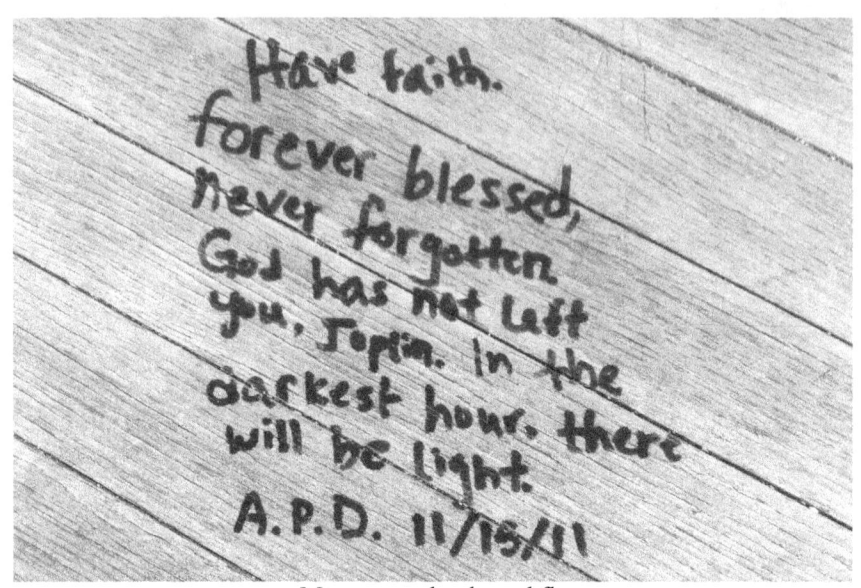

Message on hardwood floor

Message on kitchen tile

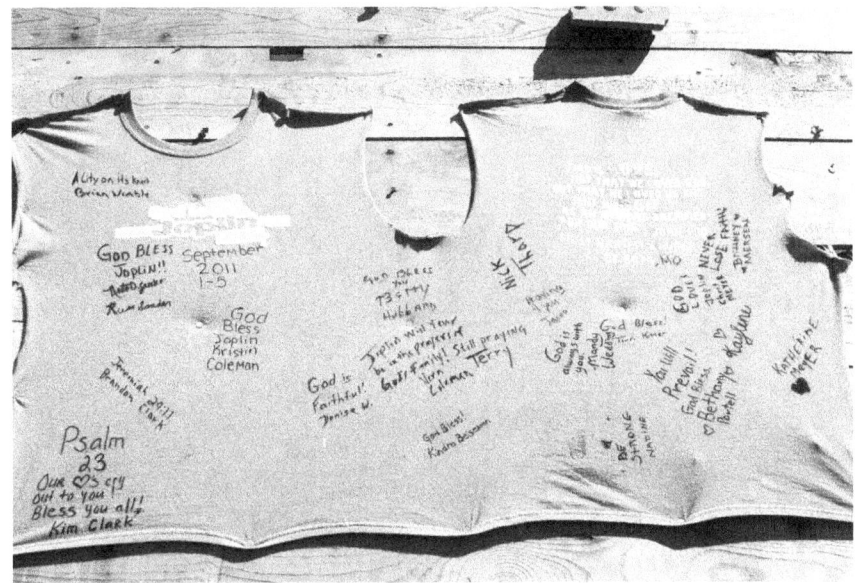

T-shirt signed and nailed to outside wall

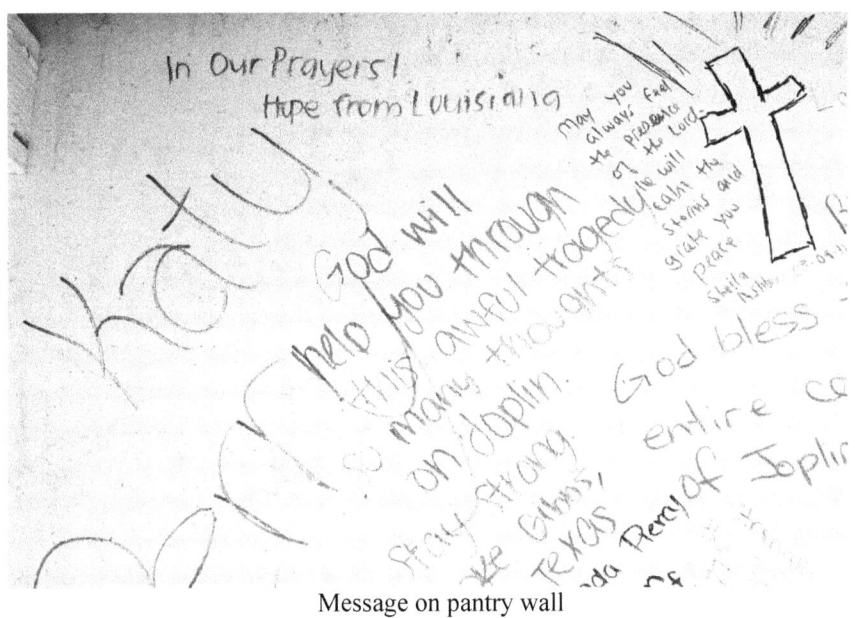

Message on pantry wall

239

Messages on closet wall

Messages on home school desktop

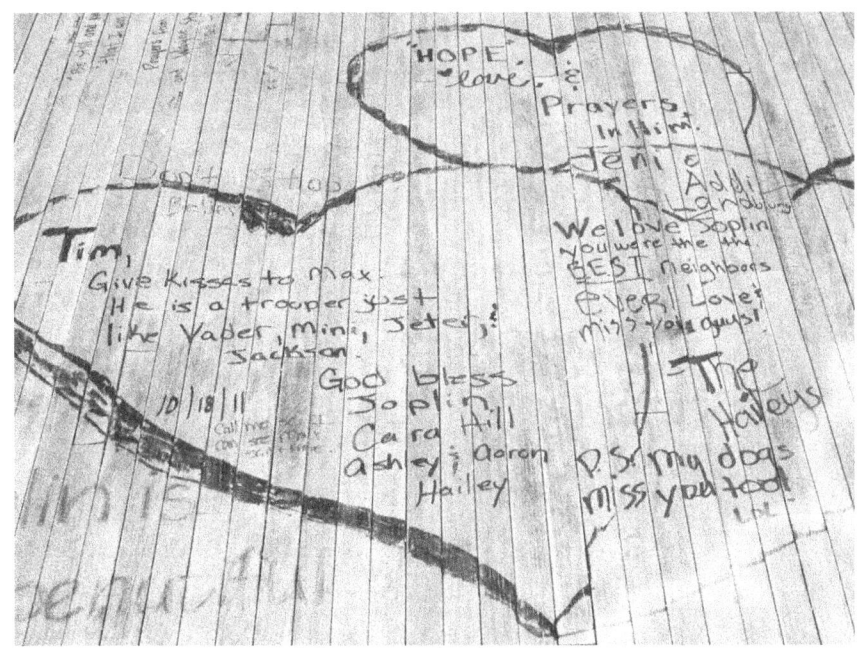

Messages on hardwood floor

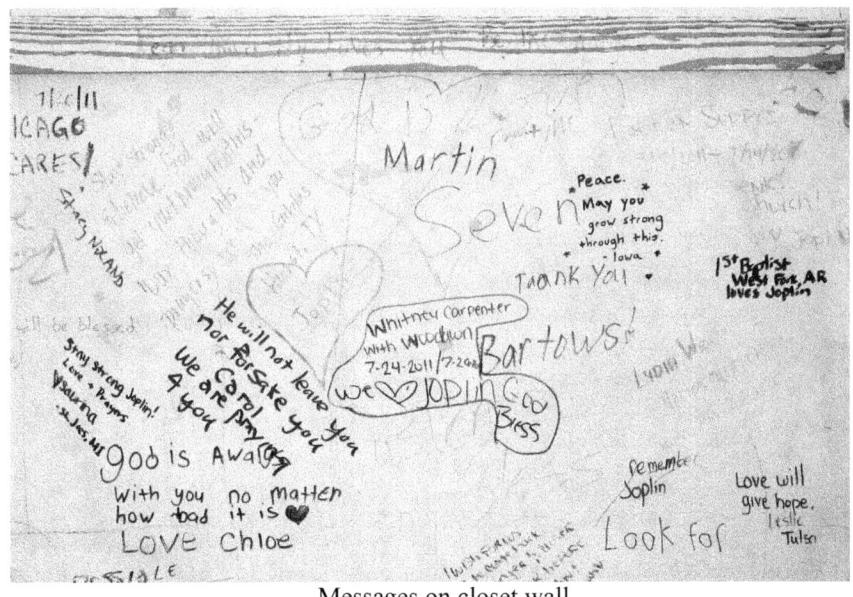

Messages on closet wall

Messages on fireplace floor tiles

Messages on bedroom wall

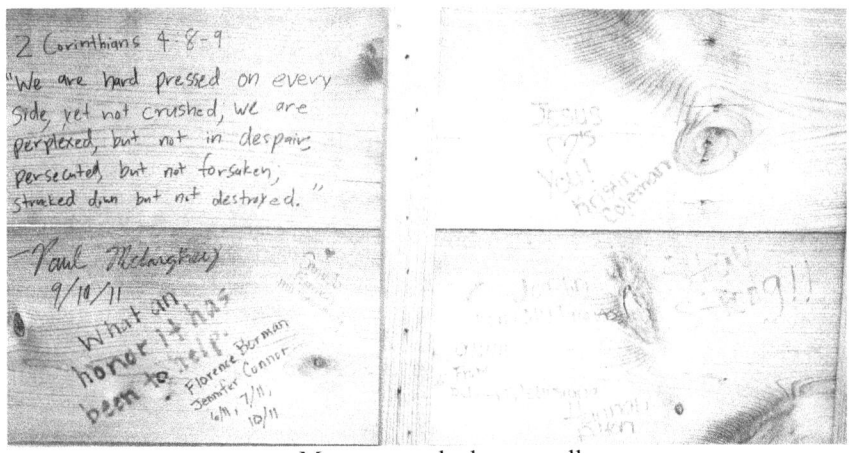

Messages on bedroom wall

Messages on bedroom wall

Messages on bedroom wall

God has blessed me
by giving you to me
as a friend...
with much love
Dawn Bass
9-10-11

Message on outside wall

244

message on outside wall

Joplin,
We have Kept You in our
prayers. We knew of the
damage the tornado caused, but
When I saw the community my
heart dropped. Now were here to help.
God Bless. If God brings you to it
He'll bring you through it. We love
you. Stay strong and keepfaith. ♥
    -Maria, Tennessee

Message on pantry wall

245

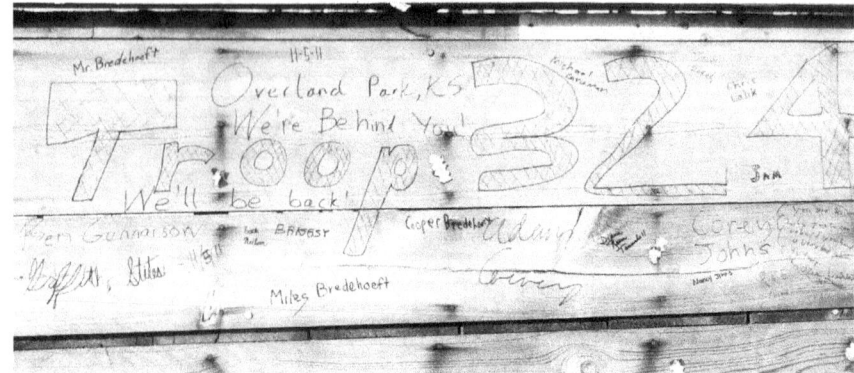

Message on outside wall

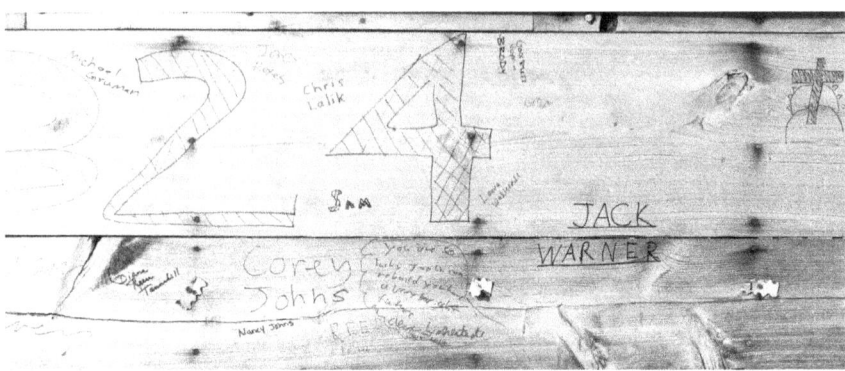

Message on outside wall

Message on outside wall

Message on outside wall

Decimated, not Defeated
Down, not Out
Twisted, not Broken
-Cody Matins
Elm

Message on bedroom wall

Message on closet shelf - Photo used with permission:
© 2011 by Gregory Fish / gregoryfish.org, All Rights Reserved

Message on closet shelf

Message on TV tray - Photo used with permission:

(more color photos, stories & information available at www.jthoh.com)

Wood walls and benches for people to sign, erected in Cunningham Park
by the Extreme Makeover Home Edition crew, reminiscent of our house

Painting on brick wall next to the convenience store / gas station

The house jacked up and off the foundation, ready to be moved

The house sitting in the street, ready to begin its journey

The house took up the entire road

Almost there

The house will sit at the city park until it moves into the museum

The empty lot where the House of Hope defied the ravaging EF5 tornado

252

**This Is
Not The End!**

**It's Just
The Beginning!**

Real Love Stories Never End!

**The Miracle of the Human Spirit
that took place in Joplin
after the tornado was driven
by the unconditional love
of the many volunteers
who sacrificed so freely
and gave so abundantly!**

**Their love and their story
will be forever preserved
on the walls of the House of Hope,
in the pages of this and other books,
in artwork and other mediums,
and the other monuments
established in their honor!**

God Bless The Volunteers!